D1800152

THINK BIG

A 10-STEP GUIDE TO ASPIRING TO GREATNESS,
PURSUING THE EXTRAORDINARY, AND
REALIZING THE FULL POTENTIAL OF YOUR
LIFE!

DAMON ZAHARIADES

ARTOFPRODUCTIVITY.COM

Copyright © 2024 by Damon Zahariades

All rights reserved. No part of this publication may be reproduced, distributed, or transmitted in any form or by any means, including photocopying, recording, or other electronic or mechanical methods, without the prior written permission of the publisher, except in the case of brief quotations embodied in critical reviews and certain other noncommercial uses permitted by copyright law. For permission requests, contact the author through the website below.

Art Of Productivity

http://www.artofproductivity.com

CONTENTS

Other Books by Damon Zahariades   v

Your Free Gift   1
Notable Quotables about Thinking Big   3
Preface   4
What You'll Learn in THINK BIG   7

PART I
**LAYING THE GROUNDWORK TO
THINK BIG**

What Does it Mean to Think Big?   15
The Rewards For Thinking Big   20
10 Obstacles Preventing You From
Thinking Big   27
Embracing Risk: A Prerequisite to
Thinking Big   39
How to Adjust Your Frame of Mind   45
Clearing Away Excuses to Unlock Your
Potential   57

PART II
HOW TO THINK BIG

Step 1: Imagine the Possibilities   69
Step 2: Turn Your Dreams Into
Actionable Goals   79
Step 3: Challenge Your Perceived
Limitations   86
Step 4: Embrace a Growth Mindset   95
Step 5: Build Your Self-Confidence
Muscles   104
Step 6: Reframe Your Narrative Identity   114
Step 7: Develop The "Take Purposeful
Action" Habit   122

Step 8: Build Your Support Team   132
Step 9: Spend Time With Accomplished
Big Thinkers   143
Step 10: Put Failure to Immediate Use   153

Final Thoughts on Thinking Big   164
Did You Enjoy Reading THINK BIG?   167

About the Author   169
Other Books by Damon Zahariades   171

OTHER BOOKS BY DAMON ZAHARIADES

How to Lead a Disciplined Life

The Mental Toughness Handbook

The Procrastination Cure

To-Do List Formula

80/20 Your Life!

The Time Chunking Method

How to Make Better Decisions

The Art of Living Well series

The Art Of Saying NO

The Art of Letting GO

The Art of Finding FLOW

The 30-Day Productivity Boost series

The 30-Day Productivity Plan - VOLUME I

The 30-Day Productivity Plan - VOLUME II

Self-Help Books for Busy People series

Small Habits Revolution

The Joy Of Imperfection

The P.R.I.M.E.R. Goal Setting Method

Improve Your Focus and Mental Discipline series

Fast Focus

Morning Makeover

Digital Detox

Visit ArtofProductivity.com for a complete list of titles and summaries. All titles are available for purchase in ebook, paperback, hardcover, and audiobook formats at ArtofProductivity.com/Amazon.

YOUR FREE GIFT

❦

I want to give you a gift. It's my way of saying thank you for your willingness to invest your time in this book. The gift is my 40-page PDF action guide titled *Catapult Your Productivity! The Top 10 Habits You Must Develop to Get More Things Done.*

It's short enough to skim but meaty enough to offer actionable advice that can make a real difference in your life.

You can get immediate access to *Catapult Your Productivity* by clicking the link below and joining my mailing list:

https://artofproductivity.com/free-gift/

You may be tempted to dismiss this gift. After all, how valuable can it be if I'm offering it to you for free? But I think you'll be pleasantly surprised. It's chock-full of tips and strategies you can use today to get more done quickly.

But there's no need to take my word for it. Join tens of thousands of other readers and judge its merits personally. I'm confident you'll find *Catapult Your Productivity* to be immediately helpful.

Damon Zahariades
https://artofproductivity.com/

NOTABLE QUOTABLES ABOUT THINKING BIG

66 If you can dream it, you can do it.

— WALT DISNEY

66 Dream big and dare to fail.

— NORMAN D. VAUGHAN, EXPLORER

66 You are the author of your own life, and it's never too late to replace the stories you tell yourself and the world. It's never too late to begin a new chapter, add a surprise twist, or change genres entirely.

— TIM FERRISS

PREFACE

~

I was a timid child.
I had dreams, like most kids at that age. I dreamt about my future and what I would become. But my aspirations were always weighed down by practicality. Rather than reaching for the stars, I was content, compelled even, to think smaller. Instead of imagining what *could* be, I thought of what would *probably* be.

Some kids dream of becoming astronauts, fighter pilots, and professional athletes. I imagined having a "sensible" job. One that paid the bills. One that was dependable and consistent. To no one's surprise, I got a corporate job when I graduated college.

Looking back, I'm convinced that thinking small shackled me to an early life of mediocrity. My ambitions and accomplishments were small. I rarely ventured outside my comfort zone, and that apprehension stunted my personal and professional growth.

One day, after much self-reflection (and frustration), I decided to change my mindset. I decided to stop thinking small. I decided to aim higher, open to what was *possible* instead of just what was *probable*.

It changed my life.

I won't lie to you. It wasn't easy. Like any ingrained habit, thinking small is a difficult one to break. The longer it ferments in the mind, the greater its hold. Progress was slow.

Eventually, my frame of mind shifted. I began pushing against the boundaries I had set for myself. I started to create bigger goals, and by a miracle of coincidence, I started to accomplish bigger things (bigger for *me*, at least).

I've seen others adopt a similar change in mindset and watched them go on to achieve remarkable feats. A friend left his comfortable, well-paying — but unrewarding — job and started a business that generates six figures each month. An acquaintance went from being a newsroom journalist, constantly stressed and under pressure, to becoming a prolific novelist, publishing 25+ books *each year*. A former colleague, once a homebody, ventured outside his comfort zone and has now traveled to more countries than I can name.

You're reading this book because thinking bigger resonates within you. At some point in your life, you've thought, "I can do better. I can achieve more."

Let me assure you, you absolutely can! It's not magic, although your results may seem magical. It's not about working harder, though hard work may be involved.

It begins with adopting a new outlook on what you can achieve. I can say with unwavering confidence that you can achieve more than you can imagine at this moment. You can accomplish extraordinary things, even if you don't believe so right now.

But there's one requirement: you must shift your mindset and adopt a new belief system about yourself. You must *believe* you can do things that might seem unimaginable. Adopting this new frame of mind may seem difficult, but it will also be rewarding. Indeed, it can be *life-changing*.

Let's go on this journey together. I'll be your guide, showing you the path that worked for me. I'll point out potholes and other hazards along the way so you'll easily sidestep them (learn from my mistakes!). And I look forward to celebrating with you the small victories you experience as we advance.

I'm excited for you! I can't wait to see your progress. But enough cheerleading (for now). Let's roll up our sleeves and get to work.

Damon Zahariades
Southern California

WHAT YOU'LL LEARN IN THINK BIG

∾

This book serves two purposes.

First, it's a step-by-step instruction manual that will show you how to think bigger today and throughout the rest of your life. It will help you develop an entirely different way of viewing the world around you. Instead of seeing roadblocks, you'll see opportunities. Instead of feeling boxed in by limitations, you'll feel liberated by new possibilities. Instead of looking at the world through a lens colored by cynicism and negativity, you'll view everything around you with optimism and enthusiasm.

These changes don't happen with a snap of your fingers. It's not as simple as flipping a switch, like turning on the light in your living room. It's a process. And the book you're reading is your procedure handbook. It'll take you through the entire process, one step at a time.

The second purpose of *THINK BIG* is to inspire you. As you learn to think bigger, you'll encounter internal resistance. That's natural. You've probably spent a fair part of your life focusing on what is practical, sensible, and feasible. Your brain is comfortable with this thought pattern and will resist your efforts to develop a more ambitious outlook. It will be reluctant to leave its comfort zone.

THINK BIG will help you counter this resistance. Simple, self-reflective exercises accompany the practical advice in each chapter. We'll turn theory into real-life results. Rather than imagining how thinking bigger can improve your life down the road, you'll see it happen in real-time. You won't toil for a payoff in the distant future. You'll enjoy the rewards of this journey now and as you progress through the chapters.

How This Book Differs from Others

THINK BIG differs from other self-improvement books in two critical ways.

First, we're not going to get bogged down in psychology. While insight into the brain's complexity is valuable, getting lost in the weeds is easy. So, we'll briefly explore some psychological theories but focus mainly on what's actionable and will produce tangible results. The quicker you experience results, the more encouraged, motivated, and inspired you'll feel to continue.

Second, the structure of this book is designed to make it easier for you to revisit select chapters according to your needs. This isn't a book that you'll read once and put away. Instead, you'll want to revisit certain sections to brush up on the concepts explained in them. You'll want to repeat select exercises to reinforce the principles they support. *THINK BIG* isn't just a book to be read, shelved, and forgotten. It's an ongoing workshop that you can return to at your leisure.

Let's take a quick look at what you'll learn in *THINK BIG*.

Part I: Laying the Groundwork to Think Big

Before moving forward to the step-by-step instruction of thinking big, we must cover some foundational principles. These principles will create the framework that we'll build upon later. They're like the basic ingredients you'd use when preparing a lavish meal. They're necessary to the final dish.

In *Part I*, we'll explore what it means to think big and examine the rewards for doing so. We'll discuss the obstacles that will try to hamper you and some of the calculated risks you'll need to take along the way. Before we close this section of the book, we'll also discuss how to change your mindset, including confronting the natural tendency to make excuses.

Part II: How to Think Big

This is where the action begins. We'll add to the framework we built in *Part I*, using it as a set of conceptual building blocks that support real-world applications. This is your roadmap. We'll shift from discussing high-level ideas and concepts to starting to take action.

In *Part II*, we'll review a detailed 10-step system for training your mind to think big. We'll break down each step, covering it thoroughly before moving on to the next one. Each step is complemented by an exercise that encourages real-world application. These exercises will help you personalize and master the skills presented throughout this section of the book.

What to Expect as You Read This Book

We're going to move through the material quickly. Many self-improvement books are unnecessarily long. They're needlessly bloated with filler, such as stories that are only tangentially related to the core material. They're padded to meet word count requirements.

Not this book. It's short. It's lean and tight. We'll cover each idea and step succinctly, spending no more time than is necessary for you to master them.

One final note before we move on: I implore you to do the exercises you'll find in *Part II*. In my opinion, they're pivotal for experiencing actual personal growth.

In some ways, the exercises are the cornerstone of the chapters they accompany.

You don't have to do them immediately. After a first read-through, you can return to the book and do the exercises at your own pace. The important thing is that you do them. They're simple, and most of them can be completed quickly.

With that out of the way, let's begin our journey.

PART I

LAYING THE GROUNDWORK TO THINK BIG

~

It's a mistake to rush headlong into any aspect of personal development without fully understanding its core principles. Doing so would be like working on a jigsaw puzzle without first dumping the pieces out of the box. It can be done, but you'll spend a *lot* of unnecessary time and effort.

To truly master the art of thinking big and reap its many rewards, we must first examine its basic premises. By exploring these concepts in advance, we'll equip ourselves with crucial insights to form the bedrock we'll build later.

This first section will shape our journey. It's an essential precursor to the techniques and strategies we'll cover in *Part II*.

WHAT DOES IT MEAN TO THINK BIG?

There is always room in your life for thinking bigger, pushing limits and imagining the impossible.

— TONY ROBBINS

L et's start by identifying what "thinking big" *isn't*. It's not about manifestation. Many people believe they can manifest the life they want by focusing their thoughts and emotions on various aspects of that life. They're confident that visualizing their desired results and harmonizing their emotions with intentionality will make their dreams come true.

Thinking big isn't about that. Yes, it begins with imagining that you can achieve remarkable things (we'll get into that in a moment). But that's merely a starting point. It's only the first step. Positivity is crucial but impotent if it isn't accompanied by purposeful action.

Thinking big starts with dreaming about what's possible. What might you accomplish in your life if you removed all of your limiting beliefs? What level of success could you achieve in your personal and professional life if self-imposed limitations didn't constrain you?

But what you do *after* dreaming about what's possible determines whether this outcome — your imagined life — becomes reality or remains a dream. This is where the real work begins.

Resisting the Pressure to be "Realistic"

As children, we were told that we could be anything we wanted. We were encouraged to view life as being full of opportunities. Adults didn't want us to feel boxed in by self-defeating assumptions.

In adulthood, this latitude vanishes. Rather than being encouraged to think big, we're pressured to be "realistic." We're urged to lower our expectations. The collective insistence of those around us can become so compelling that we eventually concede, relegating our aspirations to a small room in our mind reserved for dead dreams.

Thinking *small* becomes our norm. Unfortunately, this fuels and all but guarantees a life of mediocrity.

We must resist this pressure. It starts by recognizing

that it's easy for others to underestimate our capacity to achieve great things. In adulthood, no one will believe in us more than we can believe in ourselves. Once we recognize this fact, it becomes easier to resist the consensus that we should surrender our dreams and be "realistic."

Doing this isn't easy. Some of us must counter years of conditioning. The good news is that we ultimately control our mindset. With a structured plan, we can undo this conditioning and give ourselves the freedom to set our sights higher.

Creating Bold, Audacious Goals

In his book *Built to Last*, Jim Collins coined the acronym BHAG. It stands for Big, Hairy, Audacious Goal. It's a goal so large that it seems unreasonable or infeasible. Collins points to the Apollo 11 mission to land humans on the moon as an example of a BHAG. At the time, the idea was inconceivable. Unthinkable. Setting this goal focused the NASA team and inspired them to work together to achieve it.

Perhaps you've heard the term "moonshot." It's often used in the technology space to describe a project that is considered a "long shot." A moonshot is a brazen undertaking that requires heroic effort.[1]

Thinking big involves setting big, hairy, audacious goals for ourselves. These goals demand time, effort, commitment, and consistent, purposeful action. They require a carefully designed plan. You won't achieve these goals overnight. In fact, they might take years to accomplish. But they should inspire and motivate you. They should challenge and compel you to question and push against your self-imposed constraints.

And what happens if you don't achieve one of your bold, audacious goals? You'll still benefit greatly. While striving to reach your "stretch goal," you'll likely accomplish something remarkable. For example, imagine trying to grow your small business into an 8-figure powerhouse within ten years but only managing to generate $5 million in annual revenue by the deadline.

It's still a huge win.

Reframing Limiting Beliefs

Many of us entertain thoughts that hold us back. We tell ourselves we're not good enough, don't have what it takes, or don't deserve success. These limiting beliefs are mental roadblocks. They prevent us from achieving the success we dream about.

We accumulate and harbor these beliefs for various reasons. For example, our past experiences might have sown the seeds of self-doubt. Our cultural values may conflict with our sense of what is acceptable. Our fears of being judged by others can make us hesitant to set our sights higher than others deem reasonable. Or perhaps we're simply unaware of our capabilities because we've never tested them.

Whatever the origin of the mental obstacles, thinking

big requires us to challenge and reframe them. Are these defeating thoughts valid? And even if they contain a kernel of truth, is that kernel enough to justify the entire assertion?

For example, your inner critic might tell you, "You're too old to return to school to finish your degree." However, many people complete their degrees after spending years pursuing their careers. If they can do it, so can you.

Reframing our limiting beliefs isn't about ignoring reality. It's about questioning whether they're legitimate. We'll cover this topic in greater detail in *Step 3: Challenge Your Perceived Limitations*.

You're now familiar with what it means to think big. But why should you do it? What rewards await you if you commit time and energy to this endeavor?

---

1. This term originates from the Apollo 11 mission.

THE REWARDS FOR THINKING BIG

66 If you think small, your world will be small.
If you think big, your world will be big.

— PAULO COELHO

Everything we do begins with a reason. A desired outcome drives every action and decision we make. We go to our jobs each day to pay our bills, invest money each month to fund our retirement, and take our vehicles in for maintenance so they'll continue to work correctly.

So, why are we training ourselves to think bigger? What desired outcome justifies our time and energy spent on this training?

7 Reasons Why Thinking Big Matters

As you'll see below, thinking big has several real-life benefits. If you train yourself to do it consistently, you can
expect to reap rewards that profoundly affect your life.
Some of these rewards may not be immediately evident.
But they accrue over time. Together, they can improve
every aspect of your daily experience:

- Your career
- Your relationships
- Your family life
- Your social life
- Your finances
- Your hobbies
- Your physical fitness
- Your emotional well-being

Here are seven reasons to train yourself to think
bigger. It's not a complete list. But it'll drive home the
point that the payoff you'll enjoy is worth the investment.

Reason #1: It inspires your creativity in solving problems

You face challenges every day—in your workplace, at
home, and even while doing mundane things like shop-
ping. Sometimes, they entail personal loss, failure, or

setbacks. Sometimes, these challenges present obstacles that prevent you from attaining something you desire.

Thinking big drives you to brainstorm outside-the-box solutions to the issues you encounter. It's easier to entertain creative ideas because you're no longer constrained by conventional thinking and commonplace approaches to problem-solving.

Reason #2: It forces you to venture outside your comfort zone

Given a choice, most people prefer to stay in their comfort zones. They feel more confident and secure. Their routines are familiar, creating a safe haven that is consistent and predictable.

But this comfort comes at a steep price: you hobble your personal and professional growth. You rob yourself of the opportunity to overcome your fears and develop new skills. You deprive yourself of the chance to face adversity head-on and build resilience and the ability to adapt.

Thinking big makes you aware of these costs. It reminds you that your comfort zone is a prison of self-inflicted boundaries and limitations. A prison that holds you back even though it makes you feel protected from uncertainty. When you're aware of this fact, you're more inclined to try new things and challenge yourself.

Reason #3: It highlights your big picture

Have you ever felt aimless? Have you ever gone through your day feeling adrift and without purpose?

This happens when you neglect to associate what you're doing with what you want to achieve. For example, you go through the motions at your job without thinking about your career trajectory. You eat junk food without considering its impact on your long-term health. You attend family get-togethers and disregard the emotional connections you could nurture with your loved ones.

Thinking big encourages you to reflect on why you're doing what you're doing. It nudges you to think about your goals, urges you to consider them, and fills you with purpose and motivation.

Reason #4: It helps you to separate important from unimportant tasks

Every task and project on your to-do list *seems* important. But that's because you're too close to what you're doing. When this happens, you lose sight of the bigger picture. You lose your perspective and spend your time and energy on activities that do nothing to advance your goals. Worse, you come dangerously close to feeling over-whelmed and burnt out.

Thinking big allows you to pull back the lens. It will enable you to consider your tasks and projects in the context of your broader goals and responsibilities. It empowers you to ask yourself, "Why am I doing what I'm doing?" It challenges you to distinguish between crucial and trivial activities. It urges you to reflect on whether you're spending your time, energy, and attentional resources in a manner that will help you achieve your goals.

Reason #5: It encourages you to develop a plan

Goals without action plans are little more than dreams. No amount of positive thinking will help you achieve them if you don't create a step-by-step strategy with those outcomes in mind. No amount of optimism or enthusiasm will help you succeed if you lack a roadmap to your destination.

Thinking big motivates you to create this roadmap. It gives you a long-term vision of what you want to accomplish and pushes you to develop a course of action to get you there. It also clarifies your resources (time, energy, focus, money, etc.) and encourages you to use them judiciously. Thinking big nudges you to break down your lofty, ambitious goals into smaller goals with manageable checkpoints and milestones.

Positivity, optimism, and enthusiasm are essential. But if you want to accomplish something big, you need an execution plan.

Reason #6: It strengthens your resilience to failure

Benjamin Franklin once said, "In this world, nothing is certain except death and taxes." But he overlooked a third inescapable event: occasional failure. We experience setbacks. We make mistakes. We encounter defeat. The only way to avoid failure is never to try to accomplish anything.

Because periodic failure is inevitable, you shouldn't fear it. Instead, focus on how you respond to it. Do you allow it to paralyze you and prevent you from moving forward? Or do you see it as a learning opportunity, a circumstance you can use to improve and motivate yourself to do better next time?

Thinking big spurs you to embrace a long-term outlook. It recognizes that any road to goal achievement is sprinkled with setbacks. Any path to distant success is peppered with missteps and disappointments. Thinking big doesn't mean you'll avoid these things (there *isn't* a way to avoid them entirely). Instead, it encourages you to adopt a mindset that perceives them as opportunities to grow so you'll thrive despite them.

You'll thrive *because* of them.

Reason #7: It improves your adaptability

Adaptability and resilience to failure are interconnected. They depend on one another. When you experience failure, you learn what not to do. You learn to adapt. You try something else to produce a different outcome. This response springs from a forward-looking attitude. Rather than despair, you adjust, meeting challenges head-on.

While developing a practical lightbulb for widespread use, Thomas Edison reportedly said, "I have not failed. I've just found 10,000 ways that won't work." Edison was a big thinker who quickly adapted when his plans and efforts failed. His inventions eventually changed the world.

Thinking big makes you more resourceful. It sparks your creativity, inspiring you to come up with innovative solutions whenever you face challenges and setbacks. It urges you to adapt, arguably one of the most important skills you can develop today as the world changes rapidly.

Let's pause a moment and catch our breath. You have several compelling reasons to aim higher, dream bigger, and set loftier goals. There are additional reasons, but the ones we've covered here are (hopefully) enough to compel you to move forward.

But if thinking big is so beneficial, why don't more people do it? If envisioning yourself achieving extraordinary things can produce life-changing results, why do so many people avoid it? You'll learn the reasons in the next chapter.

10 OBSTACLES PREVENTING YOU FROM THINKING BIG

" Obstacles don't have to stop you. If you run into a wall, don't turn around and give up. Figure out how to climb it, go through it, or work around it.

— MICHAEL JORDAN

I t's easy to dream, to fantasize about success. Thinking big is more difficult because it requires intention, planning, and execution. It requires commitment and dedication. It calls for tenacity and resourcefulness. It's far more demanding than wishful thinking.

The moment you begin changing your perspective, you'll face several internal roadblocks. They'll try to slow your progress, challenge your intentions, and question why you're going through the trouble. They'll create internal resistance, fueling self-doubt and limiting beliefs about your potential and capabilities.

If you ignore these roadblocks, you'll remain vulnerable to them. They'll continue to jeopardize and stifle your development. Therefore, we must face them head-on and take steps to overcome them.

Obstacle #1: Fear about potential results

Some people fear change. Some fear failure. Some even fear success. Taking purposeful action to make your dreams a reality implies that your efforts will change your life in some observable way. Moreover, until we achieve your goals, your results and their attendant consequences remain unclear.

That can be scary.

If you fail, will others judge you? If you succeed, will you face higher expectations and be forced to take on new responsibilities? Will change make you less comfortable?

How to overcome it: Your life is dynamic. It's constantly changing, even if you don't notice. You may as well take action to influence *how* your life changes. The more action you take, the less hold this fear will have over you.

Obstacle #2: Tendency to make (and rationalize) excuses

We all make excuses, and we do it for various reasons. Sometimes, we justify inaction because we fear failure and its consequences. Sometimes, we become defensive regarding a setback to preserve a positive self-image or to influence how others perceive us. Sometimes, we create a pretext designed to help us avoid taking responsibility for an undesired outcome.

Making excuses negatively affects you. It encourages you to procrastinate. It stifles your decision-making and problem-solving skills. It weakens your confidence and undermines your willingness to act intentionally. When you make excuses, you bolster your negative and limiting beliefs about yourself. This makes it nearly impossible for us to aim high and achieve great things.

How to overcome it: Whenever you feel compelled to make an excuse, pause and ask yourself why. Are you afraid of failure? Are you trying to avoid accountability? Are you hoping to conform to others' expectations (e.g., peer pressure)? Develop this habit of self-reflection so it becomes second nature.

Obstacle #3: Pessimism

In the context of self-improvement, pessimism is a personal reflection. It's a mindset mired in self-doubt. It questions your ability to learn new information, develop new skills, and improve yourself. It causes you to mistrust your capabilities and urges you to hesitate before committing to a course of action.

When pessimism gains a foothold in your mind, it makes you reluctant to take calculated risks. Instead of imagining yourself achieving great things, you fixate on past mistakes and failures. You may even obsess over them to the point that they become part of your identity.

Pessimism erodes your motivation to do better. You become resistant to change because you assume the change will be negative. Consequently, you miss opportunities in every area of your life, from your career to your relationships.

HOW TO OVERCOME IT: Challenge every claim your inner critic makes about your abilities. For example, if it claims, "You're not smart enough," remind yourself of your past successes that contradict this claim (solving problems, earning a degree, etc.). If it claims "You'll never improve," recall times when you've learned new skills or added to existing ones.

Let no claim go unchallenged.

Obstacle #4: Aversion to taking risks

Most people avoid taking unnecessary risks. The more they have to lose, the less inclined they are to jeopardize it. Sometimes, being overly cautious makes them feel prudent. So they stay in their comfort zones, where they feel safe and unthreatened.

The problem is that you end up hobbling your potential. Your comfort zone becomes a prison of sorts. Worse, the longer you stay in it, the more difficult it becomes to escape. The perceived dangers outside your comfort zone never go away, and the less willing you are to step outside, the more hazardous the terrain appears. You become so risk-averse that aiming high and achieving ambitious goals seems unthinkable.

How to overcome it: First, acknowledge that taking thoughtful, strategic risks isn't the same as being reckless.

Second, force yourself to take small risks that carry minor consequences. If you're naturally introverted, commit to saying hello to one stranger each morning. If you've never prepared a meal, cook something simple.

As you grow more comfortable with these experiences, expose yourself to slightly more significant risks. Raise the stakes. For example, strike up a conversation with one stranger each morning. Cook increasingly complex meals. The more you do this, the more you'll whittle away your aversion to risk.

Obstacle #5: Anxiety over others' opinions

It's natural to be concerned with how others perceive you. You want people to like you and respect you. You don't want them to judge, criticize, or think poorly of you. You're a social being. As such, you feel validated by the former and embarrassed by the latter. So, you go to great lengths to meet others' expectations to encourage them to think well of you.

This effort restricts your personal and professional growth. You become so concerned about avoiding others' judgment that you fear taking risks. Your self-worth begins to be fueled by and dependent upon others' approval (both implicit and explicit). It isn't easy to think big when your self-confidence depends on how others see you.

HOW TO OVERCOME IT: Imagine that someone is disappointed with you. You feel terrible about it. Ask yourself why you feel this way. Do you feel awful because you've chosen or behaved in a manner that conflicts with your values? Or do you feel so because your emotions are unfairly tangled up with that person's approval?

Whenever you feel anxious over others' opinions of your decisions and actions, challenge whether that anxiety has merit.

Obstacle #6: Poor time management

When you fail to manage your time, your attention is hijacked by immediate concerns. Every task and project seems urgent, and there never seems to be enough time to do everything you need or want to do. You find yourself rushing from one pressing matter to another, stressed and under constant pressure. You feel like you're racing against the clock, overcommitting, and lacking the necessary resources.

This predicament severely limits your ability to see the bigger picture. It makes long-term thinking impossible because your attentional resources are preoccupied with the here and now. The demands in front of you overwhelm your focus, task prioritization, and even executive functions like goal setting, leaving you with few resources to think big. Ultimately, today's urgencies undermine your future potential.

HOW TO OVERCOME IT: First, set boundaries— personally and professionally. Get comfortable saying "no" to those who want your time. No one knows your time constraints better than you.

Second, prioritize every item on your to-do list. Give your time and energy to those that are truly important rather than merely "urgent."

Third, use time chunking to avoid distractions and focus exclusively on these critical tasks.

Obstacle #7: Perfectionism

Many people brag about being perfectionists. They take pride in being hard on themselves and holding themselves to impossible standards. But this pride is misplaced. Perfectionism erects numerous roadblocks that prevent you from achieving big goals.

It causes you to fear making mistakes, amplifying your aversion to risks. It paralyzes you, encouraging you to avoid challenges rather than take action and risk failure. Because you're less inclined to take action and risk failure, you never develop the resilience to push through setbacks. You never cultivate the grit and tenacity to take on ambitious projects and see them through to completion.

HOW TO OVERCOME IT: If you struggle with perfectionism, the first step is to acknowledge it. You must be aware of the issue before you can overcome it.

Next, permit yourself to make mistakes. Recognize that making them doesn't mean failure. Mistakes are terrific learning opportunities that can fuel your personal and professional growth.

It'll take time to get accustomed to this newfound freedom. But it's a good investment, and you may be surprised by how liberating it feels to shed your perfectionistic tendencies.

Obstacle #8: Distractibility

It's easier than ever to get distracted and lose focus. Websites and apps are designed to trigger the continuous dopamine release in your brain. Meanwhile, your calendar is filled to the bursting point with your responsibilities, obligations, and commitments. It's no wonder that your attention drifts, and you get sidetracked.

Distractions seem harmless in the moment. But the more you allow yourself to be distracted, the more susceptible you become to them. You inadvertently train yourself to entertain them, unintentionally developing a habit. Eventually, you're unable to ignore them.

When you're distracted, you can't focus on your long-term goals and aspirations. Unimportant tasks, trivial issues, and frivolous diversions grip your attention. Your stress levels climb. Your productivity and motivation plummet. Your self-discipline, creativity, problem-solving, and decision-making skills go out the window. You become less inclined to take purposeful action, and your ambitions are gradually relegated to dreams that are never achieved.

HOW TO OVERCOME IT: Start each day with a tight, focused to-do list. It should include no more than ten items and three high-priority items. (Your master to-do list can include everything that comes to mind, but keep your *daily* to-do list compact.)

Once you know what to accomplish, break your day into chunks. Block out time slots on your calendar during which you'll work exclusively on specific tasks on your to-do list.

These two measures alone will help you stay focused and engaged while keeping distractions at bay. Over time, they'll also help you break the habit of getting easily distracted.

Obstacle # 9: Imbalance between conflicting priorities

We all wrestle with conflicting interests. For example, we want to save money for retirement while indulging in nonessential purchases. We want to invest time in our hobbies but also strengthen our relationships with others.

We want to advance our careers but also devote time and attention to self-care.

Spending time, attention, and energy on incompatible priorities isn't the problem. Pursuing interests that clash with each other usually leads to a well-rounded life. The problem is failing to balance these interests. This imbalance eventually causes you to feel frustrated, discouraged, and even helpless. Your focus narrows to the point that you constantly think you're missing out on important facets of life. Allowed to grow and fester, these feelings erode your commitment to accomplishing your big goals.

HOW TO OVERCOME IT: First, identify your interests and priorities. Figure out what you need to balance.

Second, determine your constraints. This includes your time, attention, and finances.

Third, with your priorities and constraints in mind, create a plan that allocates your resources between the former.

Finally, review your results at the end of each week. Make adjustments whenever you feel things are out of balance.

Obstacle #10: Scarcity mindset

It's normal to worry whether you have "enough." Enough food. Enough money. Enough means to survive. It encourages you to be mindful of how you use your limited resources. It urges you to conserve rather than waste them.

A scarcity mindset amplifies this awareness to an unhealthy level. It causes you to *constantly* worry about having enough. Worse, this anxiety creeps into every area of your life. You worry about your relationships (e.g., are you receiving enough attention and affection?), your career (e.g., are you getting enough opportunities or accolades from your boss?), and your possessions (e.g., do you have enough clothes, gadgets, and other belongings?).

When you're consumed with worry about having enough, you become unwilling to jeopardize what you have. You're hesitant to take risks, even calculated ones, where the payoff outweighs the potential for loss. You become risk-averse, remaining in your comfort zone and playing it safe rather than attempting to achieve your large-scale goals.

HOW TO OVERCOME IT: Take stock of what you have. You probably have more than you need, even if you initially feel otherwise. For example, look in your closet. Do you see clothes that you haven't worn in a while? Look in your pantry. Do you notice ingredients that you haven't used in months?

Next, privately express gratitude for what you have. Make it a habit by doing this each morning. Finally, declutter. Nothing counters a scarcity mindset more effectively than getting rid of things you don't need.

THIS HAS BEEN A LONG SECTION, but it's vital and readies you for the road ahead. When thinking bigger and setting your sights higher, your mind is your most formidable obstacle. Awareness of the potential hurdles and road-blocks your mind will erect prepares you to deal with them productively.

We've touched on risk several times but only briefly mentioned it. It's time to dig a little deeper. Taking measured risks is pivotal in permitting yourself to chase your dreams.

EMBRACING RISK: A PREREQUISITE TO THINKING BIG

 Those who dare to fail miserably can achieve greatly.

— JOHN F. KENNEDY

E very goal you set for yourself comes with risk. Sometimes, you risk your time, money, and other resources. Sometimes, you risk your reputation. Sometimes, you risk your relationships, putting strain on your bonds with family, friends, and coworkers. You might risk disappointment, burnout, and even physical injury, depending on your goals.

Additionally, there are opportunity costs. What opportunities do you miss when you set and pursue big goals? What prospects and possibilities will you abandon to pursue your larger ambitions?

These are important questions because success is never guaranteed. Any endeavor you undertake can fail. This fact shouldn't discourage you from taking risks, of course. After all, you can only experience growth in your personal and professional lives if you're willing to take a chance on yourself. That being the case, it's important to recognize and accept the ever-present *possibility* of failure and approach risk-taking cautiously.

Why You Should Embrace Risk

You're more inclined to try new things when you're willing to take chances. This is crucial because aiming high and chasing big goals always requires stretching yourself. Sometimes, this means learning new skills. Sometimes, it means becoming more comfortable with uncertainty. Sometimes, it means jeopardizing something you value to affect an outcome you value more.

For example, going to college demands a modicum of focus and discipline. But earning a PhD calls for a higher level of both, which might necessitate training yourself to improve in these areas.

Asking someone out on a date requires a bit of courage. But asking someone to marry you and spend the rest of their life with you requires you to welcome a far greater degree of uncertainty.

Your job (hopefully) allows you to save money regularly for the future. Starting a business might require you to jeopardize your savings, using them as startup capital to pursue your dream of becoming a successful entrepreneur.

The more comfortable you become with taking risks, the more flexibility you give yourself to accomplish remarkable, even unimaginable things. Along the way, your self-confidence increases, your resilience to setbacks grows, your fear of the unknown diminishes, and you become more creative and adaptable as your circumstances change. These are some of the many rewards that accompany embracing risk.

This doesn't mean you should be irresponsible or reckless—that's tantamount to gambling. Instead, you can embrace risk cautiously and strategically with forethought, evaluation, and planning.

Calculated Risks vs. Reckless Risks

Many factors distinguish calculated risks from reckless risks, but two stand above the rest. The first is a profound awareness of a decision's potential consequences. Before you take a measured risk, you investigate and compare the upside and possible downsides. You ask yourself, "What might happen if I move forward with this decision, and how might that possibility impact me?" Then, you decide whether it makes sense to take the chance, given your desired outcome and risk tolerance.

The second factor is the degree of planning. You

research. You gather information. You seek and interview others who have taken similar risks. You devise contingency plans that are set in motion when particular outcomes occur. You do these things to help soften the impact of unfavorable results.

Contrast this approach to risk-taking with the one taken by reckless individuals. Minimal consideration is given to the potential downsides of a decision (e.g., driving while intoxicated). And even when there is a modicum of awareness, the possible downsides are usually dismissed.

Moreover, reckless individuals rarely plan their decisions. They seldom research or gather information. And they're unlikely to devise backup plans to mitigate the effects of a negative outcome. Instead, they throw caution to the wind. They act impulsively.

Risk-taking in the context of thinking big and chasing your ambitions demands thoughtfulness. It calls for caution and careful evaluation of a particular decision's possible rewards and pitfalls. It requires planning and preparation.

Taking these steps doesn't shield you from failure. Nor does it guarantee that you'll avoid making mistakes. But if you fail or make mistakes, taking these steps helps you bounce back quickly, armed with actionable insight.

Mistakes, Failure, and Gaining Insight

It's natural to worry about making mistakes. All of us dread the prospect of failure. But this anxiety is a useless obstacle that holds you back. Mistakes and failure can give you clarity and insight. They can provide perspective, keeping you humble and reminding you that you shouldn't take anything for granted.

The key is to reframe how you perceive mistakes and failure in the context of chasing your dreams. Rather than listening to your inner critic and seeing them as evidence of incompetence, you must recognize them as opportunities to learn, grow, and improve. Rather than allowing them to crush your spirit and undermine your confidence, you should use them as motivation to do better next time.

When you view your mistakes and failures through this growth-focused lens, they stop being obstacles. Instead, they become a source of actionable insight. They inform you of what doesn't work, highlight skills you need to build, and expose biases you must abandon. In this way, your mistakes and failures can serve as a springboard for self-reflection and a catalyst for purposeful action.

TRAINING yourself to embrace risk requires that you adjust your frame of mind. That's easier said than done.

You may have to unravel years of conditioning and reshape your interpretation of risks and opportunities. You may have to surrender your fear of the unknown and recognize your innate ability to adapt to changing circumstances.

We'll unpack this topic in the next section.

HOW TO ADJUST YOUR FRAME
OF MIND

" You are what you think. So just think big,
believe big, act big, work big, give big, forgive
big, laugh big, love big and live big.

— ANDREW CARNEGIE

Your frame of mind plays a pivotal role in
thinking big. It's the key that releases you from
the prison of your perceived limitations. It's the
wrecking ball that demolishes self-imposed barriers and
roadblocks. It's the muzzle that silences your inner critic,
allowing you to act boldly without fear of its disapproval.

Most people cultivate a mindset anchored by self-
doubt and fear of the unknown. Sometimes, this happens
because of their past mistakes, failures, and disappoint-

ments. Sometimes, it happens because they lack a support network; they don't have anyone in their corner encouraging and inspiring them and lifting their spirits. Sometimes, people develop a defeatist, cynical frame of mind because everyone around them tells them to play it safe. This reinforces their self-doubt and feelings of inadequacy.

When you retune how you perceive yourself and your abilities, you allow yourself to set and pursue bigger, more significant goals. You give yourself the freedom to imagine achieving things you once believed were unthinkable or impossible. You become more willing to step outside your comfort zone and take measured risks instead of playing it safe. You no longer feel obligated to conform to others' expectations.

Your mindset determines your behavior, and your thought patterns fuel your decisions. So, it's worth investing time and energy to develop and strengthen an outlook anchored by self-belief and inner confidence. One that isn't easily jarred by others' opinions. One that tolerates setbacks and uses them as motivation to press forward. The first step is to recognize the most common saboteurs.

8 Thought Patterns That Will Sabotage You

Unhelpful mental routines can quickly establish themselves if you're not vigilant. They're insidious, taking root without your notice and gradually gaining influence. By the time you recognize them, they're firmly entrenched and difficult to counter.

Here are the ones you should be most wary of, along with tips and techniques for overcoming them.[1]

1. All-or-nothing thinking

You view every circumstance, decision, and action in the extreme. There is no middle ground. You either succeed or fail.

This attitude not only discourages you from taking action but also dissuades you from entertaining the possibility that you can achieve big things.

HOW TO OVERCOME IT: When you notice yourself tagging a thought, behavior, or action (or even inaction) in binary terms of "good" or "bad," stop for a moment. Immediately challenge that thought process. Ask yourself whether it's truly the case.

For example, if you perform poorly on a school test, you might feel like a terrible student. If you make a mistake at your job, you may feel incompetent. If you cheat on your diet, you might feel like a failure.

These verdicts are never valid. Question them every time you catch yourself thinking in black-and-white terms. Don't allow them to slide by uncontested. The more regularly you scrutinize them, the less credibility they'll have when they surface.

2. Emotional reasoning

You perceive reality through the lens of your emotions. If you "feel" something is true, it's true despite a lack of evidence.

This illusion is the wellspring of self-doubt, insecurity, and defeatism.

HOW TO OVERCOME IT: Recognize when your thoughts, decisions, and actions spring from your emotions. Are you feeling angry, fearful, jealous, guilty, or sad? If so, ask yourself whether these feelings compel you to act or think in a particular way.

For example, suppose you feel afraid and assume you're in danger. You feel compelled to respond. Ask yourself whether your response is based on the facts or fueled by your fear.

Or suppose you're angry at a coworker you dislike. You're about to yell at them over a perceived slight. Ask yourself whether your anger stems from evidence of the snub or is driven by your low opinion of them.

As you develop this habit, you'll become more aware of your feelings. You'll improve at observing yourself and determining whether you think or act emotionally. The stronger this habit grows, the better equipped you'll be to approach situations objectively.

3. Catastrophizing

You exaggerate the consequences of undesirable circumstances. Minor setbacks become disasters in your mind, and small obstacles seem impossible to overcome.

This frame of mind reinforces your fear of failure and wreaks havoc on your ability to make reasonable, rational decisions.

HOW TO OVERCOME IT: Challenge every thought of disaster. Ask yourself if you possess undeniable proof that supports it. What is your evidence that catastrophe looms? When you lack such evidence, tag the thought as groundless. Be aware that you've imagined the worst possible outcome, and it's doubtful it will come to pass.

For example, suppose you need to dip into your savings to repair your home after a particularly savage storm. You start to panic that you'll never be able to save for retirement. Ask yourself if your anxiety is based on evidence and objective analysis or provoked by an exaggeration of your circumstances.

The more often you challenge your catastrophic thoughts and demand proof, the more aware you'll be of this tendency. The greater your awareness, the less inclined you'll be to fall into its trap.

4. "Should" thinking

You impose arbitrary rules regarding your actions, decisions, and behaviors. You form unjustified and inflexible expectations for yourself, your circumstances, and the people around you.

This mental habit short circuits your ability to think about what *can* occur because it fixates on what *should* occur. And when the latter fails to materialize, you feel angry, guilty, frustrated, and demoralized.

HOW TO OVERCOME IT: First, when a thought surfaces that projects your expectation, reframe it to express what you aspire to. For example, suppose you think, "I should get more exercise." Reframe this to "I would like to get more exercise." If you think, "I should be as successful as Tom," reframe it to "I'd like to be as successful as Tom."

Second, recognize your accomplishments, even those that seem inconsequential. Acknowledge your actions and decisions that align with your values and convictions. Doing this will interrupt the "should" thinking process and shift your attention to personal achievements that will motivate you, boost your self-confidence, and validate your efforts.

5. "It's my fault" thinking

You take responsibility for negative situations that are beyond your control. You blame yourself for complications, overestimating your influence over the circumstances that led to them.

This tendency impedes your ability to think big because it crushes your self-esteem, makes you feel incompetent or ineffectual, and erodes your willingness to take risks.

How to overcome it: Scrutinize every thought that insists you bear responsibility for an undesired outcome. Look for undeniable evidence that you're truly culpable. Baseless self-blame often originates from invalid presumptions regarding your degree of control over events. Demand proof from your inner critic.

Form a habit of thinking of circumstances in terms of what you can control and what you can't. This will clarify whether you're responsible for an event and to what degree.

For example, suppose you think, "It's entirely my fault this relationship deteriorated." This assumption is probably untrue. Some things were in your control, but it's likely some things weren't. By identifying both, you'll interrupt the mental habit of erroneously assuming everything is your fault.

6. Negative Labeling

If you make a mistake, you tell yourself that you're incompetent. You consider yourself a failure if you try something and miss the mark. If there's room for positive change in your life, you fixate on your shortcomings, building your identity around them. You brand yourself with negative labels (e.g., "incompetent," "failure," etc.).

This thought pattern creates a negative self-image, which anchors your actions and decisions. You become fearful of criticism—from others and your inner critic. You begin to doubt yourself, staying in your comfort zone rather than facing challenges head-on.

How to overcome it: Reevaluate your expectations. Negative labeling often stems from perfectionism. We impose impossibly high standards on ourselves and criticize and demean ourselves when we fail to measure up to them.

Be aware of when you assign negative labels to yourself. If labeling has become a habit, it likely happens on autopilot, meaning it goes unnoticed. To reverse this cognitive process, you must first recognize when it happens and challenge the label.

For example, imagine that you make a mistake at your job and immediately think of yourself as a failure. Challenge the legitimacy of this self-judgment. Does your mistake genuinely make you a failure, or does everyone occasionally make mistakes? The more you question the negative labels you assign yourself, the less credible they'll become.

7. Discounting the positive

When you accomplish something, you trivialize your role. When someone compliments you, you play down your involvement. When they congratulate you, you shrug it off.

This mindset erodes confidence and your sense of agency. You inadvertently train your mind to disregard your potential. Over time, the prospect of achieving your big ambitions starts to seem unthinkable.

HOW TO OVERCOME IT: To reverse this negative thought pattern, write down every accomplishment right after it occurs. Detail the accomplishment and everything you did to make it happen. No accomplishment is too small to record.

This only takes a moment. Keep a journal handy for convenience. If you spend most of your day in front of a computer and prefer to record everything digitally, do so.

This journal helps in two ways. First, it'll help you to recognize a tendency to devalue your actions and decisions. At first, taking credit for the things you've recorded may feel uncomfortable. It might seem as if someone else did them. This instinctive reaction exposes the habit, which might slip under the radar unnoticed and unchecked.

Second, your journal will counter the discounting reflex. Every time you review it, you'll be reminded that you made particular outcomes happen. You set things in motion. You engineered your success. No matter how small, these past achievements will contradict the notion that you played a trivial role.

8. Playing the victim

You blame unfavorable circumstances on external factors you claim to have no control over. Setbacks occur because life isn't fair or others treat you poorly. Failure hounds you because you lack the resources you need to succeed.

This way of thinking urges you to avoid taking responsibility for your role in the situations you find yourself in. It "protects" you from feeling accountable.

How to overcome it: Recognize this thought pattern as a false narrative and be aware of when you entertain misstatements associated with it. Then, challenge these misstatements by asking yourself whether your actions and decisions contributed to them.

Do this in a loving, self-compassionate way. The goal isn't to criticize yourself for mistakes. The goal is to develop a sense of agency and self-empowerment and look for ways to grow and improve.

For example, suppose you want a job promotion but are passed over. You might instinctively think the following:

- "My boss and colleagues hate me."
- "My skills and talents aren't appreciated here."
- "There's no way to advance at this company."
- "The only way to get ahead is to brown-nose."
- "My coworkers are holding me back."

First, think about each of these statements. Ask yourself whether they're true. In most cases, they won't accurately reflect your circumstances. Not entirely, at least.

And not to the point of being 100% responsible for your situation.

For instance, one or two coworkers might dislike you, but that alone won't ruin your chances of getting a promotion. It may not be easy to advance, but it's likely possible without trying to curry favor by brown-nosing.

Second, review your situation and ask yourself if your actions and decisions played a role. Do you complete projects late? Do you contribute ideas during important meetings or remain silent? Are you defensive when you receive constructive criticism? Do you go above and beyond or do the bare minimum?

Again, don't focus on self-condemnation. Instead, use this to bolster your sense of personal agency. Acknowledge the power of your choices and actions and recognize your ability to shape your future.

Doing this interrupts the victim mentality. Repeating it every time you're tempted to credit unfavorable circumstances to external factors reinforces a new narrative that highlights your ability to determine your path.

It's impossible to imagine yourself accomplishing extraordinary things when these paralyzing thought patterns hobble your headspace. The good news is that you *can* triumph over them. You can reshape your mental habits by incorporating the practices outlined above.

It won't be easy. Most of us have spent years—even

decades—unwittingly reinforcing these mental saboteurs. Reversing them will be challenging. It'll require time, energy, and lots of patience and self-compassion. But there's no better time than the present to start the process. And the rewards for doing so can genuinely be life-changing.

---

1. I'm using "you" in an inclusive sense to speak to common mental habits many people struggle with. My intention isn't to imply blame but rather to make these counterproductive tendencies more relatable to the reader and encourage change.

CLEARING AWAY EXCUSES TO
UNLOCK YOUR POTENTIAL

“ We have more ability than willpower, and it is
often an excuse to ourselves that we imagine
that things are impossible.

— FRANÇOIS DE LA ROCHEFOUCAULD

We all make excuses. We justify our lack of
success, rationalize our inaction, and
excuse our indecision. We tell ourselves
why we'll never achieve our ambitions, even when we
know our reasons are merely a pretext for
procrastination.

It's tempting to dismiss this tendency and overlook its
detrimental effects. Knowing everyone does it is reassur-

ing, and this consolation makes us less inclined to confront it. For many people, the tendency becomes a habit. It becomes instinctual, a knee-jerk response to any thought—any hope—of achieving great things.

The problem is that making excuses creates a breeding ground for other bad habits. We procrastinate. We avoid accountability. We blame others for personal setbacks and disappointments. We start to doubt ourselves, questioning our abilities and potential. We become less inclined to leave our comfort zones. And so rather than setting our sights high, recognizing our potential, and chasing our dreams, we settle for less in every area of our lives.

Let's put an end to this counterproductive habit. Below, we'll examine some of the most common excuses we tell ourselves in various contexts.

Common Excuses We Tell Ourselves

We often make excuses without realizing that we're doing so. This oversight allows the behavior to become habitual, forming unnoticed and growing under our radar. By reviewing often-used excuses in different scenarios, we'll see how easily this tendency can become a part of our routine.

You may have made some of these excuses at some point in your life or even today. That's okay. No judgment. Our purpose is to recognize how making them chips away at our sense of self-agency and our motivation to think big.

Diet & Exercise:

- "I don't have time to exercise."
- "I don't have time to cook meals at home."
- "I've tried to lose weight, and it didn't work."
- "I can't afford to buy healthy food."

Career / Business:

- "I don't have the right connections to get ahead."
- "I don't have the skills I need to be promoted."
- "I'm too busy to take courses or attend workshops in my field."
- "My boss has it out for me."

Self-Improvement:

- "I'm too old to make changes in my life."
- "I don't know what to do or how to go about it."
- "I've tried to improve myself in the past, and it didn't last."
- "I don't have the willpower."

Personal Relationships:

- "I don't have time to meet new people."
- "I don't know how to start a conversation."
- "I've had bad experiences and don't want to get hurt again."
- "I'm too shy."

Academic Pursuits:

- "I'm not smart enough to get a degree."
- "My job doesn't leave me enough time."
- "I was never good at school."
- "I'm too old to go to college."

Passion Projects (e.g., cooking, learning to play the guitar, writing a book, etc.):

- "I don't have the resources to commit to it."
- "I don't have anyone to teach me."
- "I'm not talented enough."
- "I have too many other responsibilities."

Again, if you've made any of these excuses in the past, cut yourself some slack and extend yourself some grace. What matters most is that you recognize how the *habit* of making excuses erodes your enthusiasm and resolve to chase your dreams.

Why We Make Excuses

Before we can curb this habit, we need to recognize why we do it in the first place. How did this habit develop? What factors stimulated it? What factors reinforced it? Once we've determined these things, we can address them head-on. The following are the most common reasons we make excuses.

PROCRASTINATION—This allows us to delay taking action without feeling as if we're giving up. The *intention* to act is there, but it's always in the future.

FEAR OF FAILURE—This is related to procrastination. If we never take action, we never have to confront failure. That is until we realize that perpetual inaction is its own kind of devastating failure.

PAST DISAPPOINTMENTS—We associate taking action with undesired outcomes. We lose confidence in ourselves, and success begins to seem unattainable. We delay taking action to avoid having to face failure once again.

INNER CRITIC—This negative internal voice tries to convince us that we're not good, talented, or smart enough to succeed. The more we listen to it, the more credible it seems. We start to believe it.

PERFECTIONISM—We rationalize our inaction by claiming that we're waiting for the right time or until we're prepared. This habit stems mainly from the impossibly high standards we set for ourselves.

CHALLENGE AVOIDANCE—We enjoy the security of our comfort zone. Stepping outside of it exposes us to challenges that disrupt this sense of security.

GOAL AMBIGUITY—We delay taking action because we're uncertain what we want and how to achieve it. This lack of clarity justifies — in our minds, at least — our unwillingness to move forward.

Now that we're aware of the most common reasons we make excuses, we can start working to overcome this habit.

Fair warning: This work isn't easy and will not be completed overnight. But if we start now, we can chip away at this self-defeating pattern. Gradually, we'll conquer it and, in the process, give ourselves the freedom to act with boldness, optimism, and self-confidence.

How to Stop Making Excuses

I will quickly share several things you can do to break the excuse-making habit. We'll need to unravel years of conditioning, and our minds will resist change. So, be prepared to show yourself patience and compassion. It will take time to break this deep-seated pattern and replace it with a healthier one.

The most important thing you can do is to recognize that making an excuse is making a choice. You *choose* to do nothing rather than take action.[1] You *choose* to procrastinate rather than move forward. You *choose* to justify and rationalize rather than take responsibility and hold yourself accountable.

This sounds harsh, but it's actually liberating. Once you acknowledge that you're in the driver's seat, you admit to yourself that you can make different choices. You can decide to overcome your tendency to make excuses. You can choose to unlearn your conditioning and replace self-sabotaging patterns with self-empowering ones.

Here are seven things you can start doing today to break free of the excuse-making habit.

1. When you feel like procrastinating, take small actions rather than worrying about the larger undertaking. If you want to exercise, just put on your running shoes. If you want to write a book, write one or two sentences. Focus on progress rather than completion.

2. When you fear failure, reframe the risk as an opportunity to learn and improve. If you're a freelancer and launch a service that fails to attract interest, you've gained valuable insight.

3. When you find yourself dwelling on past setbacks, don your investigator's hat. What went wrong? If you had to do it again, what would you do differently? How would you avoid a similar outcome in the future?

4. When your inner critic rears its head, challenge its claims. Did you genuinely experience a catastrophe or just a minor setback? Are you truly incompetent or simply unprepared, a state you can easily rectify? Are you legitimately unworthy of success and happiness, or is your inner critic exploiting limiting beliefs fueled by the past?

5. When you feel paralyzed by your inner perfectionist, give yourself permission to make mistakes. Embrace imperfection, recognizing that every mistake provides a chance to learn and improve.

6. When you feel like staying in your comfort zone, commit to taking on a new challenge. Instead of grabbing a quick meal at your favorite fast-food venue, prepare a simple meal at home. Instead of keeping to yourself when standing in line, strike up a conversation with the person in front of you. If you're invited to a party, say yes instead of no.

7. If you're unsure what you want to accomplish, clarify your goals. Break them down into small steps. Review what you need to acquire (skills, supplies, etc.) and actions you need to take to accomplish these steps. Create a plan that specifies milestones and deadlines.

These seven tactics are simple. You can implement them today. But remember, the excuse-making habit is an ingrained behavior. It uses a neural pathway formed when the habit took hold, which has been reinforced with repeated use. Rewiring things will take time.

The upside is that reversing this habit counters many other self-sabotaging habits, such as procrastination and perfectionism. Starting this work today will pay dividends throughout the rest of your life.

WE'VE COVERED a lot of material in *Part I: Laying the Groundwork to Think Big.* It was necessary because thinking big requires a dramatic shift in how we perceive ourselves, our capabilities, and our potential. For most of us, our self-perception has been undermined and hobbled over the years, sometimes starting during childhood.

The good news is that you can gradually deconstruct fallacious thought patterns that fuel your negative self-image and create new, healthier ones to replace them. It takes work, but you can do it. You can recondition your behaviors and responses. You can rewrite the counterproductive script that plays in your head—a script that holds you back from achieving the success you crave and deserve.

Once you do so, setting your sights higher, creating

bigger and more audacious goals, and taking action *expecting* to achieve them will become second nature.

---

1. As in the previous chapter, I'm using "you" in a general sense.

PART II

HOW TO THINK BIG

~

It's time to put everything we've discussed into motion. In this section, we'll build on the foundational aspects of thinking big addressed in *Part I*.

I'll take you through a step-by-step process to train your mind to see beyond any self-imposed boundaries currently holding you back. This detailed roadmap includes steps that involve only you, as well as a few that involve others. As you'll learn, the accountability, encouragement, and emotional support from involving others in this journey are invaluable.

Each step is accompanied by a targeted exercise designed to reinforce the ideas presented and give you an opportunity to implement them. These exercises are crucial parts of the learning process. They'll give you real-world experience applying the concepts you learn and deepen your appreciation for how these concepts fit into the framework we'll build together. I encourage you to do them at a pace that suits you (I've provided estimations of the amount of time each exercise will require).

It's "go time." Let's roll up our sleeves and get to work.

STEP 1: IMAGINE THE POSSIBILITIES

66 Think little goals and expect little achievements. Think big goals and win big success.

— DAVID. J. SCHWARTZ

As children, everything seems possible. We can
become anything we want, achieve whatever
we set our minds to, and go wherever our
imaginations lead. And nothing seems impossible if the
people we look up to—our parents, older siblings, teachers, etc.—encourage this mindset.

At that tender age, the world is truly our oyster.

As we grow older, our perspective changes. All of the
things that seemed possible during childhood begin to
seem unattainable. Our dreams become tempered by our

experiences. Our aspirations are shelved as we focus on our obligations and responsibilities. The light of our imagination diminishes. It may even go out, like a spent candle's dying flame.

We learn to accept our current circumstances as an endpoint of sorts, a plateau rather than a springboard to bigger things.

The first step to training ourselves to think big is to rekindle that fading optimism. It's still in our minds' attics, neglected and covered by dust and cobwebs. We're going to bring it back to life and restore it to its former glory. It begins with reminding ourselves of what is possible.

The Art of Possibility Thinking

We tend to see the world through a lens focused on what we *can't* do. Our mindset is hedged in by our perceived limitations. Our lack of self-belief constrains our outlook. We see our shortcomings as insurmountable, minimizing our skills and talents.

Possibility thinking turns this frame of mind on its head. It prompts us to look beyond our perceived limitations and shortcomings. It urges us to consider that our futures are not set in stone. Where we once saw only problems, we now see solutions. Where we once noticed only roadblocks, we now spot cleared paths to previously abandoned destinations.

To practice possibility thinking, we must stop fixating

on what we believe to be *impossible*. First, we need to quiet our inner critics, the loudest voice telling us what can go wrong or why something is infeasible. We can do this using three tactics at every opportunity:

1. Challenging its dubious claims
2. Reframing self-defeating thoughts as constructive feedback
3. Recalling our past accomplishments

Second, we must accept that others' opinions are fallible. This includes opinions from friends, family members, coworkers, and even seasoned experts. Their perspectives are often hobbled by their own negative thinking. Consider that Thomas Watson, chairman and CEO of IBM, famously said in 1943, "I think there is a world market for maybe five computers."

Once we've abandoned the negativity around us, refusing to let it dictate our potential, we must develop the habit of asking questions about what is possible. We can do this in myriad ways during a given day.

For example, suppose you're waiting in line to purchase goods at your local grocery store. The line is long and slow-moving. Ask yourself how you would solve this problem as the store's manager. You could open more registers, modify your employees' work schedules to accommodate higher foot traffic, or encourage your employees to handle customers' goods more efficiently.

Or suppose there's a workflow bottleneck in your

department at your job. Ask yourself how you would solve this issue if you were in charge. You could identify the people involved and offer to reassign the nonessential tasks on their plates. You could reallocate resources. You could use automation or upgrade software.

You may be thinking, "How does this help me to think big?" By asking these types of questions throughout the day, in whatever situations we find ourselves in, we train our minds to think about possibilities. Each time we do this, we erode our tendency to think of reasons why something *can't* be accomplished. We're developing the *habit* of possibility thinking. Over time, this habit will compel us to instinctively think of how to achieve things — even things we may have once believed to be beyond our reach.

One last technique for embracing the art of possibility thinking is to study the accomplishments of high achievers. These can include people alive today (or recently passed) and throughout history.

Examples of the former might include Steve Jobs, Bill Gates, Michael Jordan, George Lucas, and Richard Branson. Examples of the latter might consist of Martin Luther King, Jr., Albert Einstein, Joan of Arc, Wolfgang Amadeus Mozart, and Napoleon Bonaparte. These people achieved remarkable feats, some at an astonishingly young age. They can serve as a rich and constant source of inspiration when we think of what might be possible for us.

The Art of Visualization

Visualization builds on possibility thinking and uses it as a springboard. Once we've considered what's possible, we imagine ourselves achieving those outcomes. We picture ourselves making decisions and taking purposeful action, confronting and overcoming challenges, and ultimately accomplishing the goals we desire to achieve.

World-class athletes use visualization while preparing to compete. They mentally rehearse performing specific actions well. For example, basketball players envision themselves making flawless shots under pressure from various spots on the court. Football players picture themselves carrying the ball securely past the opponents as they run toward the goal line. Tennis players conjure up images of returning serves with perfect form and aim.

Visualization is attached to sports psychology for many reasons. Some of them align with our reasons for practicing it:

- It conditions our minds for successful outcomes.
- It increases our self-confidence as we repeatedly call up images of ourselves doing what's required to succeed.
- It eases our fear of uncertainty and failure.
- It focuses our attention on what we need to do rather than what can go wrong.

- It relaxes our minds, alleviating the stress and anxiety accompanying the pressure to perform well.
- It helps us make better decisions and finer-tuned plans by clarifying our goals and clearing our mental clutter.

So, how do you get maximum mileage from visualization? How do you get started, and how can you practice it to get the most out of it? Here are my suggestions, all of which proved helpful for me:

1. Find a quiet spot that's free of distractions, and get comfortable. Wear headphones if you can't escape the noise in your immediate environment.
2. Start by closing your eyes and taking a few deep breaths to calm your mind and purge your mental clutter.
3. Picture yourself making every decision and performing every action that leads to accomplishing your goal.
4. Involve your sensory pathways. View the scene in your mind as you strive toward and achieve success. Smell it. Hear it. Feel it. Taste it.
5. Do it at the same time every day. Make it a part of your daily routine. I do it in the

evenings before going to bed. Choose a time that works best for you.

6. Keep your visualization sessions short (e.g., 5 minutes)—at least in the beginning. Lengthen them as you become more comfortable with the practice.

7. Record your experience in a journal. Jot down how you felt. Note any mental roadblocks or distractions.

It took me a long time to fully embrace visualization. It seemed "flighty" to me. However, once I began to practice it regularly, I understood why world-class athletes swear by it.

EXERCISE #1

THIS EXERCISE HAS TWO PARTS. The first part will help you put possibility thinking into action, and the second part will address visualization.

Part 1

Write down every area of your life where you'd like to improve. I recommend using pen and paper because the tactile experience of writing stimulates brain activity.[1] But do what feels most comfortable to you. Here's a quick list of categories to consider:

- Career
- Finances
- Relationships
- Fitness
- Mental health
- Education
- Hobbies
- Spirituality
- Self Improvement
- Languages
- Travel

Use this list as a catalyst to brainstorm areas of your life. Add additional areas as they come to mind.

Next, reflect on each item that appears on your list. For each one, jot down one audacious goal. Don't worry about whether it seems realistic.

If your inner critic claims that the goal is infeasible, demand evidence. If past disappointments come to mind, reframe them as feedback to help you succeed. Then, recall past successes that suggest you can accomplish your goal.

For example, suppose you earned a bachelor's degree in economics and immediately got a job instead of continuing your education. Your goal might be to return to school and earn a Ph.D. in economics.

If your inner critic claims your goal is unachievable, challenge the claim. Insist on seeing evidence. If this negative voice brings memories of doing poorly in school, reframe these memories as learning opportunities. What changes can you make to improve outcomes (e.g., study more consistently, spend more time preparing for tests, etc.)? Then, recall that you earned a bachelor's degree. You have what it takes to finish the race.

Go through this process for each area of your life that you included on your list.

Part 2

Find a quiet place where you can focus without distraction. Sitting comfortably with your list before you, close your eyes and take a few deep breaths. Clear your mind of the day's minutiae, and let go of any stress or anxiety you're feeling.

Next, open your eyes and review your list. Choose one of your audacious goals. Close your eyes again and visualize every step you need to take to achieve your goal. Picture yourself taking those steps.

Involve your senses. See yourself in situations and circumstances related to your goal. Envision yourself doing everything you need to do to finish the race.

Let's return to our example of earning a PhD in

economics. Visualize yourself completing assignments, reading economic literature, conducting research, analyzing data, and preparing for exams. Form a mental picture of meeting with your professors and discussing the curriculum. Picture yourself creating the framework of your thesis and gathering the resources you'll use to write it.

If this is your first visualization session, keep it short.

Finally, record your experience in a journal. I recommend using a simple note-taking app, such as UpNote, OneNote, or Evernote, so you can review your entries whenever you like across all your devices.

Time required for Part 1: 10 minutes.
Time required for Part 2: 5 minutes.

---

1. Umejima, K., Ibaraki, T., Yamazaki, T., & Sakai, K. (2021). Paper Notebooks vs. Mobile Devices: Brain Activation Differences During Memory Retrieval. *Frontiers in Behavioral Neuroscience, 15.* https://doi.org/10.3389/fnbeh.2021.634158

STEP 2: TURN YOUR DREAMS INTO ACTIONABLE GOALS

66 A dream written down with a date becomes a goal. A goal broken down into steps becomes a plan. A plan backed by action makes your dreams come true.

— GREG REID

∿

Quick recap…

You've brainstormed the possibilities for every important aspect of your life. You've visualized yourself realizing your dreams in these areas. Now, you've arrived at a fork in the road. Will you allow your dreams to remain mere wishes and desires, or will you formulate plans to accomplish them?

Goal setting is a pivotal factor when it comes to thinking big. In some ways, it's the most important. Sadly, many people neglect to set goals and struggle to transform their dreams into the outcomes they desire.

This section will be easy if you're experienced with setting goals and have a firm grasp of the process. On the other hand, if you rarely set goals or are unfamiliar with how to do so properly, this section will serve as a crash course.

Nothing Happens Without First Setting a Proper Goal

Recall a time when you were motivated to accomplish something big. You were excited. You were inspired, even. Maybe you wanted to lose 100 lb. Perhaps you dreamed of becoming fluent in a second language. Maybe you hoped to start a business that would become the dominant player in your field.

Did your aspiration fade away as time went on? Did it fail even to get off the starting block? If so, you're not alone. We can all relate to this experience.

Our dreams can wither away for many reasons. Sometimes, we consciously allow them to as other areas of our lives become more important and take precedence. We put our dreams on the back burner or abandon them entirely. But often, our dreams evaporate because we neglect to set action-oriented goals to help us achieve them.

When we set goals correctly, we give ourselves direction, clarity, and purpose. We create a roadmap that shows us the path forward. We set milestones to measure our progress and help us to stay on track (or get back on track when we deviate from it).

When we neglect this process, our path forward is unclear. We drift aimlessly, lacking a compass. We might genuinely feel motivated and inspired but perpetually struggle with indecision and inaction. We procrastinate, unsure of how to get started, much less how to advance. Eventually, our dreams die on the vine.

The good news is that you can entirely avoid this problem. All you need to do is devote time to careful planning and thoughtful strategizing. I'll show you how below.

How to Turn Your Dream Into an Action Plan

There are many ways to set goals. One of the most popular approaches is creating S.M.A.R.T. goals, prioritizing five parameters. A "smart" goal is specific, measurable, achievable, relevant, and time-bound (notice the first letters spell "smart"). It's a sound system.

I prefer to use my P.R.I.M.E.R. method. It's more comprehensive and addresses a couple of shortfalls inherent in the S.M.A.R.T. system. Here's what each letter of the acronym represents:

P = Pinpoint your high-priority ambitions
R = Refine your desired outcomes

I = Identify the actions you'll need to take
M = Modify your environment to complement your goals
E = Evaluate your progress
R = Revisit your goals

Let's quickly unpack this 6-part framework.

First, if you have many big goals, it's important to rank them in terms of their importance to you. You must prioritize because your time, energy, attention, and money are limited resources.

Once you rank them, consider the ones at the top of your list. Why are they your top priorities? How would your life change if you achieved them?

Second, fine-tune your desired end result. Goals are often hazy in the beginning, but this step brings them into focus. For example, you might want to "transform your physique." But that goal is vague. Refine it by determining your desired weight, lean muscle mass, fat composition, and muscle definition in your upper and lower body.

Third, create a detailed roadmap that leads to your refined results. This roadmap will specify everything you need to do. Using our example, it would include a diet plan and workout regimen. It would also feature a timeline with milestones to track your progress.

The best way to create this roadmap is to work backward. You know precisely what you'd like to achieve. Start there and determine the immediately preceding milestone. Then, assign a deadline to achieve it. Do this over and over until you've worked back to the present.

Here's a simple example: suppose your body fat percentage is currently 45%. You'd like to get down to 8%. Decide to achieve a 10% body fat percentage by a particular date. Then, decide on 12% by a specific date. Then, 14%. And so on. Extend this series of milestones back to the present.

Fourth, change your environment to accommodate your goal. Environmental factors play a major role in goal achievement. Continuing with our example, throw out the junk food in your pantry. Buy a set of kettlebells so you can exercise without going to a gym. Buy kitchen supplies to cook meals at home.

The fifth step is easy. Regularly check whether you're hitting your milestones according to your self-assigned deadlines. If you're not, revise your roadmap to accommodate your progress.

Finally, revisit your goal periodically and ask yourself if it's still important. It's easy to get tunnel vision, pursuing things that are no longer relevant or feasible due to a change in priorities or circumstances. If your goal is no longer a priority, don't be afraid to abandon it. That'll free up your limited resources to pursue higher-priority ambitions.

To summarize, many people confuse their aspirations with goals. They assume that entertaining the former is the same as creating the latter. But that's not the case at all. Forward-thinking, strategic goal-setting separates fantasy from real-world success. Its absence is one of the most common reasons people fail to achieve their desires.

∾

EXERCISE #2

∾

THIS EXERCISE FOCUSES on the third and fourth steps detailed above. We'll refine a vague goal and create an action plan to achieve it.

First, choose a short-term goal. Although thinking big entails setting huge goals, *small* goals are better suited for our purpose here.

Next, fine-tune this goal. Be very specific about what you want to achieve. For example, instead of trying to "lose weight," you might decide to "lose 18 lb." Instead of trying to "save money," you might decide to "save $4,500."

Now, create a roadmap. Start with your desired result and work backward. Include milestones and assign a deadline for each one. Here's an example roadmap for saving $4,500.

Today's date: January 1st
Final deadline: $4,500 by July 31st
Milestone #5: $3,750 by June 30th
Milestone #4: $3,000 by May 31st

Milestone #3: $2,250 by April 30th
Milestone #2: $1,500 by February 28th
Milestone #1: $750 by January 31st

The main purpose of this exercise is to develop the habit of being specific about your goals and creating detailed action plans to achieve them. We're using small goals for this exercise, but once you form the habit, you can easily apply this process to your massive goals.

Time required: 20 minutes.

STEP 3: CHALLENGE YOUR PERCEIVED LIMITATIONS

 There is no man living who isn't capable of doing more than he thinks he can do.

— HENRY FORD

We maintain an inward-focused belief system regarding our skills, talents, and potential. We cultivate this framework throughout our lives, starting during childhood. Many things influence it—both positively and negatively.

Your belief system about yourself can inspire and embolden you to accomplish remarkable things in your life. It can give you the resilience you need to press forward when you face challenges and setbacks, confident you'll overcome them.

On the other hand, it can also serve as a prison. If your self-perception is fueled by negative thoughts, harsh criticisms, and self-imposed limitations, you'll find it almost impossible to entertain, let alone pursue, big goals. Each limiting belief about yourself is like a chain that binds you to a life of mediocrity.

The third step in learning to think big is confronting your self-limiting thoughts. We'll tackle them head-on, challenging their legitimacy. When they prove to be unfair or unfounded, we'll confidently jettison them. But first, let's quickly explore how these thoughts arise in the first place. This will inform our strategy for refuting them.

The Origins of Your Self-Critical Thoughts

Numerous influences can cause a negative self-image to form and flourish. Unfortunately, these influences are not always apparent to us. This lack of awareness allows them to harm our mindset, unnoticed and unchallenged.

Sometimes, they're subtle, whispering and gently nudging our subconscious to embrace self-criticism. Sometimes, they're overt, hypercritical, and overly judgmental. Both result in self-doubt and can even lead to varying degrees of self-loathing. Here are the most common sources of these self-critical thoughts.

FAMILY—Maybe your family belittled you when you were young (perhaps they still do so). Maybe they negatively compare you to siblings who have excelled in their respective fields. Perhaps they conditionally express their love and affection, making you feel you must constantly earn these things. Your family can have a devastating effect on how you perceive yourself.

AUTHORITY FIGURES—Authority figures can have a similar impact when you're young. Your teachers may have criticized your intelligence. Your coaches may have disparaged your athleticism. Your bosses may have routinely questioned your competence. These interactions shape your beliefs regarding your potential and capacity for success.

PAST FAILURES AND MISTAKES—We discussed both earlier and will do so again in Step 10, so we won't belabor the point here. Suffice it to say, holding on to past failures and mistakes, blaming yourself rather than learning from them and letting them go, feeds feelings of guilt and shame. These feelings wreak havoc with your belief in your ability to accomplish big goals.

OTHERS' EXPECTATIONS—Other people's unreasonable expectations can make you feel inept and inadequate. If you allow these expectations to dictate your actions, you'll constantly struggle with these feelings. Over time, they'll wreck your self-esteem to the point that you can no longer imagine achieving anything but the smallest goals.

UNFAIR COMPARISONS—These days, it's easier than ever to compare yourself to other people, usually in a negative context. The pervasiveness of image-based social platforms only amplifies this tendency. You observe others (supposedly) living your desired life and feel inadequate because you're not living that life yourself.

INNER CRITIC—Your inner critic exploits the above influences. It uses them to create and maintain an internal monologue that continuously denigrates your abilities and undermines your potential.

This sabotaging dynamic has gone on long enough and done enough damage. Let's finally challenge your inward-focused negative belief system and reshape how you see yourself.

How to Banish Self-Critical Thoughts and Overcome Your Self-Imposed Limitations

There's no sense in sugarcoating this. Reversing self-sabotaging beliefs will take time, energy, and patience. It'll require self-reflection and self-compassion. You'll not only unravel years of negative conditioning but also wrestle with your brain's resistance to change.

It's not enough to sidestep these mental roadblocks; they must be torn down. Here's a multi-pronged approach, using self-directed questions as prompts.

"What limiting beliefs are holding me back?"

You must be aware of your self-imposed limitations before you can challenge them. Limiting beliefs often fly under the radar. They do their best work when they're undetected and operate without rebuke.

Asking yourself this question will help reveal the limitations you're placing on yourself.

"What evidence supports these perceived limitations?"

The internal dialogue telling you that you're not good enough, not smart enough, too old, too young, or unready to achieve great things must be challenged at every turn. Otherwise, it will continue to belittle you. That's its job.

But remember, the burden of proof remains on your inner critic. Ask for evidence, and you'll probably discover that its criticisms are meritless.

"What boundaries should I create to protect myself?"

Not everyone in your life will support your goals and aspirations. Some will be downright negative, opining on why you won't succeed. They may even do this believing they're doing you a favor. Some mean well even as they siphon away your self-confidence, enthusiasm, and optimism.

Protect yourself by erecting personal boundaries. Limit the time you spend with negative or toxic people. Decline to share your ambitions with them. When they opine about your abilities, don't engage with them. Let them have their say, and then gracefully detach from the conversation.

"What external expectations am I trying to meet?"

It's easy to fall into the trap of molding your actions, decisions, and behavior to meet others' standards. Your family. Your friends. Your coworkers. Your neighbors. Those who share your culture. Society itself. The tendency to try to measure up can become so ingrained that you do it without thinking about it. Without questioning whether you *should*.

You are not obligated to please other people or meet their expectations. Aside from your reasonable commitments, the only person you should strive to satisfy is yourself.

"Am I comparing myself to others?"

Comparing yourself to others *can* be helpful when you use the comparison as a catalyst to plan and act purposefully. For example, you observe a friend with strengths and circumstances similar to your own accomplish something you want to achieve. You then use that observation to inspire and motivate yourself to do the same.

However, outside of this limited context, comparing yourself to others is unhealthy. It breeds jealousy and resentment, stirs up self-doubt, and causes feelings of inadequacy. Asking yourself this question will help you focus less on others' achievements and more on your own journey.

"What past failures are causing me to doubt myself?"

Every road to success is littered with mistakes and failures. It's easy to let these experiences fuel your limiting beliefs, particularly if success remains ahead of you. Memories of them are typically hazy, which allows your inner critic to exploit them to reinforce its litany of criticisms and judgments.

This question will spotlight past experiences that are undermining your confidence. It'll lay them bare so you can scrutinize them objectively, learning valuable lessons from them rather than letting them feed your self-doubt.

EXERCISE #3

THIS EXERCISE IS simple and easy. We're going evaluate a limiting belief that's fueling your perceived limitations.

Our purpose is twofold. First, we want to bring this self-critical thought to the forefront so it can no longer operate incognito. Second, we want to challenge it, determining whether it has merit or is unsupported by evidence.

The first step is to identify one of your self-defeating thoughts. Ideally, it'll be associated with something specific you'd like to accomplish. Here are a few examples:

- "I'm too old to start a business."
- "I'm not disciplined enough to get into shape."
- "I don't have what it takes to earn a Ph.D."

The second step is to figure out the origin of this negative self-assessment. Where did it spring from? Did it form due to your family's constant belittling of your abilities and potential? Did it develop as a result of past failures and mistakes? It's possible that multiple factors contributed to it. Write down all of them.

The third step is to evaluate each item you've written down and examine the emotions each one evokes. For example, you might feel angry, hurt, embarrassed, and resentful when your family disparages you. Set these emotions aside for now. Detach yourself from them.

Finally, review the limiting belief you identified in the first step and evaluate it objectively. Does the evidence prove that it's legitimate? Or is it fueled primarily by the negative emotions you've associated with it? If evidence exists, are you giving it more weight than it deserves based on these emotions?

You'll probably find that your limiting belief is built on one or more faulty premises. Once you've exposed it as such, you'll be able to abandon the perceived limitation it feeds more easily.

Time required: 15 minutes.

STEP 4: EMBRACE A GROWTH MINDSET

 Life is not about finding yourself. Life is about creating yourself.

— GEORGE BERNARD SHAW

The term "growth mindset" has been a catchphrase for years. It's routinely mentioned in business schools, management workshops, sports training, and leadership conferences. It's also regularly mentioned when discussing entrepreneurship, mental toughness, and emotional health. It's practically a rallying cry in the self-improvement space.

There's good reason for this, particularly for thinking big. When you develop a growth mindset, everything becomes achievable. You can learn how to do something you don't currently know how to do, improve if you struggle in a particular area of your life, or use constructive feedback to do better down the road.

With a growth mindset, there's always room for improvement. That's integral to chasing your dreams. Nothing seems impossible when you know you can get better at anything. You start to see obstacles as challenges rather than roadblocks that hold you back. You begin to see setbacks and failures as opportunities to learn new insights rather than reasons to quit. You instinctively look for ways to adapt to difficult situations rather than giving up in frustration.

Below, we'll compare and contrast the growth mindset with its counterpart, the fixed mindset. Along the way, you'll see how the latter undercuts all attempts to think big. Then, we'll cover several things you can do immediately to develop the former.

Do You Have a Fixed Mindset or a Growth Mindset?

Your self-image stems from one of two core mindsets. Both greatly influence your actions, decisions, and general behavior. They decide your willingness to set huge goals. They dictate your motivation and enthusiasm to pursue your ambitions with intention and confidence. They determine your resolve to actualize them and inform your tenacity to keep moving forward when things go wrong.

A fixed mindset presumes that your talents, abilities,

and intelligence are fixed at birth. It is accepted as a given that you can do nothing to change these things. You can't improve. You can't better yourself. You can't rise above who you are at this moment.

Consider what this means in the context of thinking big, setting huge goals, and aspiring to do great things in your life. If you hold onto a fixed mindset, you'll be inclined to:

- Give up when you experience setbacks
- Steer clear of challenges to avoid failing and seeming inept or ineffectual
- Become defensive when given constructive feedback
- Fixate on achieving tiny goals at the cost of personal growth
- Compare yourself to others and feel threatened by their success
- Assume there's no reason to try since trying to improve is pointless

This self-perception precludes aiming high and chasing your dreams. It presupposes that your potential is capped early in life. It assumes your abilities, and thus prospects, flatline at a certain level, and trying to accomplish more than that level "allows" is futile.

Now, contrast this to a growth mindset. This perspective assumes that your talents, abilities, and intelligence can continually expand. You can learn and improve. You can develop and master any skill.

Consider what *this* means in the context of thinking big. If you maintain a growth mindset, you'll be inclined to:

- Persevere when you face setbacks
- Look forward to challenges because you feel they'll teach you something useful
- Welcome feedback as an opportunity to develop or refine your skills
- Focus on the bigger picture instead of chasing tiny goals, fixated on trivial outcomes
- Feel motivated and inspired when you see others succeed
- Embrace hard work, confident that your efforts will make you proficient and lead to success

Notice how the growth mindset aligns perfectly with setting ambitious goals and envisioning yourself accomplishing extraordinary things. The growth mindset is integral to thinking big. It'll inspire you to venture beyond your comfort zone. It'll motivate you to create lofty goals with every intention of achieving them. It'll give you the self-confidence to tackle challenges and break through obstacles.

With this in mind, how do you build a mental framework focused on personal growth rather than limitations?

How do you change your way of thinking so that you can finally recognize your potential?

How to Cultivate a Growth Mindset

You can easily replace a fixed mindset with a growth mindset. Fair warning: Making any worthwhile change in your thought patterns will require time, effort, consistency, and patience. But rest assured that you *can* do it if you follow a carefully planned strategy. Here's a 4-step blueprint.

Step 1

The first step is to identify signs of a fixed mindset. It's easy to overlook them. Moreover, the longer you've entertained a fixed mindset and the more ingrained the attendant beliefs, the more desensitized you likely are to them.

For example, do you instinctively shy away from tasks, projects, and other endeavors that seem challenging? When you struggle, do you blame external factors rather than recognizing your shortcomings? When people offer helpful feedback, do you become defensive and dismissive?

Don't punish yourself if you notice these or any other red flags. The purpose of this first step is to become aware of the issue. Spotting the telltale signs of a fixed mindset makes the problem less abstract and more tangible.

Step 2

Next, acknowledge that every action starts with a choice. Anything and everything you do begins with a decision to do that thing.

For example, if you confront a roadblock and give up, you do so because you've *chosen* to give up. If someone offers you feedback and you embrace it to improve, you do so because you've *decided* to embrace their input.

When you acknowledge that your actions arise from your choices, you admit you're in the driver's seat. You accept responsibility for what happens immediately *after* you confront challenges and setbacks. You recognize that you're accountable. While this might seem scary, it's empowering. You're in control. You determine your path forward.

Step 3

Get into the habit of perceiving failure as an opportunity to learn something useful. Because this is easier said than done, breaking this step down further is helpful.

First, realize that everyone experiences failure. The most successful person you know has gone through it many times. From world-class athletes and bestselling authors to successful entrepreneurs and accomplished leaders, all of them have faced it. Failure is universal.

Second, whenever you fail, ask yourself the following questions:

- "What can I learn from this?"
- "What factors led to this outcome?"
- "Which of my decisions contributed to it?"
- "Knowing what I now know, how would I do things differently?"

This isn't a fun process. But it can lead to valuable insights you can use to effect better outcomes.

Third, constantly remind yourself that failure isn't a final ruling on your abilities or capacity for success. It's not a verdict about your potential. On the contrary, failure is merely a signpost that points toward lessons to be learned and skills that can be improved.

Lastly, surround yourself with people who will be supportive and encouraging when you fail. You don't need people who will merely commiserate with you. Instead, you want to be around those who will motivate and inspire you to press forward. You want to spend time with people who will boost your spirits and cheer you on when you encounter setbacks.

If you do these things regularly, your brain will gradually reframe how it perceives failure. This is a crucial aspect of thinking big, and we'll discuss it in greater detail in *Step 10: Put Failure to Immediate Use*.

Step 4

Seek challenges. Welcome them with open arms. The more challenges you accept or pursue, the more opportunities you'll have to identify personal shortcomings. This means you'll have more chances to fine-tune your skills or develop new ones. You'll have more chances to develop proficiency in select areas of your life.

This step is fourth for a reason. If you haven't gone through the preceding steps, being made aware of your shortcomings will be unpleasant and perhaps even distressing. That's counterproductive. But once you've reframed how you perceive failures and setbacks, this step becomes a more rewarding experience. Pessimism is replaced by optimism. Habitual negativity is replaced by a positive attitude and enthusiasm to learn and improve.

Cultivating a growth mindset isn't like flipping a switch in your brain—not even close. It's a remapping of your thought patterns. It isn't easy. It takes time. You'll be unraveling years of conditioning, so be patient with yourself. I promise you will successfully develop a growth mindset if you follow the four steps above.

≈

EXERCISE #4

≈

THIS IS A SIMPLE JOURNALING EXERCISE. I recommend doing it the old-fashioned way: with pen and paper.

Each time you encounter a setback, write down the

incident in your journal. Then, ask yourself the following questions and record your answers.

- What feelings did I experience?
- What beliefs fueled those feelings?
- Did I have a positive or negative attitude regarding my ability to adapt?
- Was I tempted to give up, or did I feel compelled to persevere?
- If I was tempted to give up, what emotions and thought patterns contributed to the temptation?

This exercise aims to improve your self-awareness regarding your mental tendencies. As you follow the four steps outlined above and regularly do this exercise, your outlook will shift. You'll see fewer and fewer signs of a fixed mindset as you observe and embrace your potential to learn and improve.

Time required: 10 minutes per journal entry.

STEP 5: BUILD YOUR SELF-CONFIDENCE MUSCLES

 Stand up straight and realize who you are, that you tower over your circumstances.

— MAYA ANGELOU

We spend a lot of time thinking about how others see us. That's natural—even healthy. We're social beings and want to feel connected to other people. When we're around strangers, this tendency helps us feel as though we belong. When we're around loved ones, it deepens the sense of intimacy we share with them.

But sometimes, this tendency goes too far. Left unchecked, it begins to eclipse how you see yourself.

Others' perception of you takes precedence. You gradually lose your sense of identity as you spend your time and energy struggling to meet the standards others set for you.

This wrecks your self-confidence over time. You start relying on other people for validation, which triggers your self-doubt. You begin to fear disapproval from others, which paralyzes you with inaction. You allow others' appraisal of you to dictate your decisions.

It is impossible to think big without self-confidence. How can you chase your dreams and turn them into reality if you lack faith in your abilities? How can you set and achieve ambitious goals if you underestimate yourself and mistrust your instincts?

In *Step 4*, we cultivated a growth mindset. Regarding developing self-confidence, we're already halfway there. Let's finish this part of our journey.

Signs That You Struggle With Self-Confidence

Self-doubt isn't always obvious. It may be entirely camouflaged if you seldom venture outside your comfort zone. If you only do things you do well, those proficiencies can give you a false sense of security. It's a form of confidence built on a shaky foundation. It's a mirage that evaporates when you challenge yourself and encounter difficulties.

So, let's probe deeper by reviewing several traits and tendencies that suggest a lack of confidence. Don't be concerned if some of them resonate with you. We'll discuss how to overcome them in a few minutes.

INDECISION—You worry about making bad choices because you don't trust yourself to make good ones. You doubt your interpretation and appraisal of relevant information, and you end up second-guessing yourself.

PROCRASTINATION—You feel perpetually unprepared to take action. You're uncertain you have what it takes to succeed, so you put off moving forward. You haven't given up but can't get off the starting block.

PERFECTIONISM—You obsess about doing things perfectly. You set impossible standards for yourself and fear being unable to measure up to them. The possibility that you'll make mistakes causes you to hesitate and may even paralyze you with inaction.

LOW EXPECTATIONS—You set low expectations for yourself to avoid disappointment. A part of you expects to fail, and lowering your expectations shields you from negative emotions triggered by failure. This tendency discourages you from setting and pursuing ambitious goals.

IMPOSTER SYNDROME—You feel unworthy of the success you've experienced. Despite clear evidence of your abilities, talents, and resilience, you feel as though your success is unearned. This feeling haunts you, spurring you to work harder while you fear being exposed as a fraud.

NEGATIVE SELF-TALK—Your inner critic constantly criticizes your decisions, actions, and aspirations. When you fail, it makes you feel incompetent. When you succeed, it makes you feel undeserving. Nothing is good enough to satisfy it.

DISMISSIVE OF COMPLIMENTS—You're skeptical when others say nice things about you. You take their praise with a grain of salt because you struggle to feel worthy of it. You avoid the limelight of others' acclaim, expecting to disappoint them.

SENSITIVITY TO FEEDBACK—You feel insulted when others give you constructive criticism. You feel demeaned and undermined when you receive less-than-stellar feedback. Such feedback discourages you rather than motivates you to learn, adapt, and improve.

AVOIDANCE OF RISKS—You stay in your comfort zone because it's familiar and certain. You play it safe, telling yourself that doing so is prudent. This caution provides stability but also causes you to miss opportunities.

FEAR OF FAILURE—You're reluctant to try new things because you worry they may lead to a negative outcome. Every challenge carries the specter of failure, which makes you feel helpless and paralyzed, unable to move forward.

DEFLECTION OF RESPONSIBILITY—When confronted with a mistake, you refuse to be held accountable. Rather than admitting fault, you shift the focus onto others, hoping they'll receive the blame.

LACK OF BOUNDARIES—You have difficulty saying no and setting healthy boundaries. You feel your time, energy, and other resources are less important than other people's. You sacrifice your own needs to avoid conflict.

Again, don't be alarmed if you notice any of the above traits in your life. We all have experienced them. None of us is born with self-confidence. It is something we learn to adopt and embrace throughout our lives.

If you lack self-confidence, you've been conditioned to feel that way. Numerous factors may have contributed, many of which you had no control over. The critical thing to note is that you can recondition yourself. You can adjust your self-image and build your self-confidence muscles.

It's not easy, but the rewards are significant. You'll cultivate the courage and grit to face adversity head-on. You'll foster a deep-seated conviction in your abilities and potential. You'll develop inner strength and enjoy a sense of personal empowerment that encourages you to set challenging goals, confident that you can achieve them.

A Quickstart Guide To Improve Your Self-Confidence

Here's the good news: there are many simple activities that you can do each day to build your confidence. Think of them as exercises similar to those you'd do to develop and hone your physical muscles. Here, we're building your *confidence* muscles.

The key is to do these activities consistently. You won't develop self-confidence overnight. But if you take daily action and focus on making steady progress, you'll find that it grows faster than you might imagine.

Let's get started.

Take Risks

Step outside of your comfort zone at least once each day. This might sound overly simplistic, but spending all day in the safe space of familiar territory is easy. *Too* easy. So, commit to doing something that feels awkward or daunting.

Greet a stranger if you're shy. Try a new recipe if you seldom cook. Offer to teach someone a skill if you usually avoid leadership roles.

Be Decisive

Practice making snap decisions. Start with small ones where the stakes are small, and the consequences are negligible.

Choose a restaurant for you and your friends. Accept or decline invitations to social gatherings without hemming and hawing. Reply to emails and texts quickly. Doing this will train you to rely on your instincts.

Guard Your Space

Create personal boundaries and stick to them. Don't set multiple boundaries all at once. Create one at a time.

If you dislike people dropping by your home unannounced, let them know. If you dislike people invading your personal space and being physically clingy, let them know. If you dislike people involving you with their unnecessary drama, let them know.

Be tactful and diplomatic. And be prepared to assert yourself when others resist.

Seek Feedback

Ask someone you trust to evaluate something you've done. Encourage this person to be candid but kind. Express that you're looking for constructive feedback so you can improve.

Cook a meal for a friend and ask for their opinion. Share a piece of writing with a family member and ask them to critique it. Make a pitch to your boss and ask them to provide input. Doing this will desensitize you to criticism.

Journal Your Wins

Record your successes. You experience small wins throughout each day. Jot them down. No win is too small to be included.

Maybe you made a phone call that you had been dreading. You fixed a problem with your computer. You ate a healthy lunch instead of indulging in junk food. Make a quick note in your "achievement journal."

Whenever you feel self-doubt creeping in, open your journal and review your wins. You might be surprised by how inspiring and confidence-inducing this practice is.

Build Your Support Network

Surround yourself with supportive people. Spend time with people who listen to you and encourage you. Those who show empathy when you experience setbacks but inspire you to press onward. Those who offer you advice when solicited and do so without judgment. Those who *believe in you.*

Conversely, withdraw from people who regularly criticize, shame, undermine, and manipulate you. The rewards for maintaining those relationships are slim, perhaps even nonexistent. Worse, they can have a devastating and lasting impact on your self-confidence.

If you do these activities daily, you'll find it increasingly easier to believe in yourself. Do them for an extended period daily, and your self-confidence will grow by leaps and bounds. Remember, self-confidence isn't a light switch. You can't just turn it on. It forms slowly and builds over time.

Once these "muscles" become strong, feats that used to seem unimaginable will no longer seem so.

∾

EXERCISE #5

THIS IS A SIMPLE JOURNALING EXERCISE. It'll not only build your confidence, but it can also be fun. In this exercise, you'll answer three questions.

QUESTION #1: What small wins did I experience today?

Did you complete a difficult task at your job? Did you spend quality time with your family? Did you take your car in for maintenance? Did you fix that leaky faucet at home? Did you call a client you've meant to call for a while? No win is too small. Jot all of them down.

QUESTION #2: What daily habits have I purposefully maintained over the last 30 days?

Have you been visiting the gym according to your planned workout schedule? Have you been keeping a consistent morning routine? Have you been waking up earlier each morning? Have you been decluttering your workspace at the end of each day?

QUESTION #3: What milestones have I achieved over the last 12 months?

Did you lose a certain amount of weight? Did you receive a promotion at your job? Did you learn basic conversational skills in a new language? Did you read one personal development book each month?

This journaling exercise highlights your ability to accomplish the goals you set for yourself. It'll inspire you to believe in yourself whenever you step outside your comfort zone.

Time required: 30 minutes.

STEP 6: REFRAME YOUR NARRATIVE IDENTITY

 We are not what happened to us, we are what we wish to become.

— CARL JUNG

~

Your brain has created a narrative about you. It's informed by everything you've experienced throughout your life and everything you imagine will happen to you. It includes people you've met, problems you've faced, and situations you've found yourself in. It incorporates character arcs, themes, and plots.

It's called a narrative identity. It heavily influences how you perceive yourself, motivating and inspiring you to think big or sapping your morale and enthusiasm.

Your brain has developed this narrative to help you make sense of your life. To interpret everything that has ever happened to you in the context of what it implies about your future. Where does your path lead? Are you destined for success or failure? Will you accomplish big things, or are you meant to live a life of mediocrity?

The critical thing to note about this inner narrative is that it's just a story. It's autobiographical, but in the same way that a movie is "based on true events." It's not entirely factual, and so it's not wholly reliable. And here's the most crucial point to keep in mind…

You can reframe your narrative identity.

Your story is not set in stone. Your potential hasn't been determined. It continues to evolve daily as you experience new events, meet new people, develop new skills, take new risks, and overcome new challenges. Your narrative changes as your beliefs about yourself shift and grow.

This is excellent news because it gives you control. It puts you in the driver's seat, where you can reshape your story however you choose.

How to Reshape Your Narrative Identity

If you want to rewrite the story your brain tells about you, revisit the experiences that inform that story. Scrutinize them. Interrogate them. Your emotions influenced your interpretation of those events while you were experiencing them. Revisiting them gives you an opportunity to see them in a new light. It allows you to observe them through the lens of objectivity.

You'll be able to determine better whether the themes your brain created are legitimate. You'll be able to tell whether the meanings your brain has associated with them and the lessons you've learned from them are valid. If they're not, you can challenge them.

That's how you reshape your narrative identity. That's how you rewrite your story from one mired in feelings of failure and inadequacy to one fueled by personal agency and empowerment. That's how you replace a defeated and demoralized self-image with the belief that anything is possible.

Think about the pivotal moments in your life that you view through a negative lens. The crossroads where you had to make consequential decisions — and made ones that led to undesirable outcomes. The milestones you needed to achieve to move forward — and failed to achieve. The transformative events that shaped your narrative in a way that discourages you, even today, from chasing your dreams.

Investigate each of these moments. Ask yourself whether your perception of them is justified or an alternative viewpoint is more reasonable. Are the meanings and lessons you took from these incidents valid, or are there other insights and takeaways that frame a more positive self-image?

For example, suppose you had aspired to start a business years ago but abandoned the idea. Further, suppose your brain associated the incident with feelings of laziness, incompetence, or hopelessness. These negative feelings shaped your narrative. They informed the story about who you believe yourself to be.

But are they legitimate?

Is it possible that you postponed starting your business because you were trying to advance your career at the time? Were you starting a family that needed your energy and attention? Did you analyze your situation at the time and decide to wait based on your circumstances and access to resources?

These alternative views create a different narrative. They frame a story with themes highlighting your ambition to succeed, loyalty to your family, and ability to make rational decisions. They question your brain's interpretation of the event and help to reconstruct the account in a more positive, encouraging, and inspiring light.

When you revisit past experiences, you get to change how you view them. You get to short-circuit the inner monologue that's quick to point out perceived faults and inadequacies unjustly. You get to replace it with a monologue that emphasizes your abilities and talents, capacity for growth, and potential for success.

Change Your Self-Image By Changing Your Self-Talk

Your inner voice can be a toxic companion. It points out your mistakes. It questions your competence. It undermines you at every turn. If a friend or colleague treated you this poorly, you'd sever the relationship.

Unfortunately, you can't part ways with this unpleasant sidekick. That would be akin to outrunning your shadow. But you can break free of its toxicity and turn it into an ally. You can replace its constant criticism and judgment with positive self-talk that reshapes how you see yourself.

First, notice whenever you make a negative statement about yourself. Don't ignore it, even if it has become so common that you're accustomed to it. Pause a moment and recognize it. See it for what it is. If your inner voice repeatedly makes the same claim, write it down.

Second, challenge the claim immediately. Is it rational? Does evidence support it? Or is it an overreaction or overgeneralization? Is there any reason to believe the claim is legitimate? Plato once said, "silence gives consent." Don't accept your inner critic's claims in silence.

Third, come up with a positive counterargument for each negative statement. For example, if your inner voice says, "You have nothing to be proud of," respond by pointing to your accomplishments. If your inner voice claims, "You're not worth loving," counter by noting the people who love and care about you.

Fourth, focus on your efforts to change your circumstances. Your inner voice's claims are presented as a snapshot of your current situation. But remember, your story isn't entirely written. You're growing. You're improving. You're learning new things. You're making progress and moving forward. So if your inner voice says, "You're fat," respond by pointing out that you're taking action to change that circumstance. If your inner voice claims, "You're uneducated," counter by noting your plan to earn your degree.

Over time, your self-image will transform. You'll notice your abilities and potential rather than fixate on your flaws and shortcomings. Your self-confidence and self-belief will grow, and you'll no longer be shackled to the false narrative identity your brain and inner voice manufactured.

You'll develop a *new* narrative. A new story filled with fresh prospects and exciting possibilities for your future. A story that grows with you rather than being stunted by a faulty interpretation of your past experiences.

EXERCISE #6

IN THIS EXERCISE, you'll create a forward-thinking personal narrative. It will include your ambitions and values, hopes and dreams, and the character traits you aspire to build while pursuing them. This narrative will describe the person you want to become and define your ideal self.

This isn't a work of fiction; it's a work of *optimism*.

First, jot down 10 of your core values. These are the principles that influence your behavior, decisions, and actions.

Second, write down your top 5 long-term ambitions. These are the big goals you have your heart set on.

Third, reflect on and record the attributes you'd like to adopt. These are character traits that align with your values and ambitions. Here are a few examples:

- Courage
- Creativity
- Persistence
- Compassion
- Self-discipline
- Mental toughness
- Focus
- Leadership
- Assertiveness
- Decisiveness
- Patience

The final step is the most fun. Use your imagination to construct a self-image built upon everything you've written down. See yourself embodying your values and principles and using them to guide your decisions and actions. Picture yourself pursuing and achieving your ambitions. Visualize yourself developing and demonstrating your desired character traits.

This new self-image will differ from the one attached to your current narrative identity. That's the purpose of this exercise: Gradually let go of an unjust, baseless narrative and build a new one that springs from imagining the possibilities. One that's more positive, optimistic, confident, and compassionate.

One that inspires you to think bigger and presume that your ambitious goals are feasible.

Time required: 25 minutes.

STEP 7: DEVELOP THE "TAKE PURPOSEFUL ACTION" HABIT

66 Inaction breeds doubt and fear. Action breeds confidence and courage. If you want to conquer fear, do not sit home and think about it. Go out and get busy.

— DALE CARNEGIE

This is the secret ingredient.

While thinking big is primarily about aiming high, setting lofty goals, and imagining yourself accomplishing spectacular things, nothing happens unless you put your plans in motion. Nothing occurs until you take purposeful, consistent action. This is what distinguishes a dream from success. It transforms a fantasy into reality. It turns an aspiration into a tangible outcome.

Taking purposeful, consistent action does much more than this, however. It also gives you momentum. Action begets action, with small strides forward leading to bigger ones. It also mitigates your fears and eases your self-doubt. Taking the initiative focuses your attention on goal achievement rather than worrying about the unknown. It also leads to valuable lessons and insights that can only be acquired after you get things rolling. These insights are the seeds of your continual growth and improvement.

Taking purpose-driven action consistently is difficult for most people. It doesn't come naturally, and it's more comfortable to do nothing than to face the risks that accompany being proactive.

This is the reason for developing a "take action" habit. It's too important to leave to the fickle nature of motivation. When taking deliberate, goal-oriented action becomes a habit, it's easier to move forward, feeling enthusiastic and optimistic rather than overwhelmed and underprepared.

It's easier to think big with *intention*.

Reasons You Avoid Taking Action

To create this habit, you should be aware of the obstacles that stand in your way. This includes the thought patterns and mental tendencies that have discouraged you from taking decisive action in the past. Here are the most common, a few of which we've already discussed (albeit in a slightly different context):

PAST FAILURES—You started a business that went bankrupt. You started a relationship that ended in heartbreak. You took the initiative at your job only to fumble and lose a promotion. These experiences make you doubt yourself and question whether it's worth being proactive.

FEAR OF INADEQUACY—You worry you're not up to the task. You're anxious that you don't have what it takes. This fear paralyzes you, trapping you in a state of inaction.

IMPOSTER SYNDROME—You attribute your past achievements to luck and other external factors. You feel your success is undeserved, and you're fearful others will discover you're a fraud. This concern discourages you from moving forward.

OTHERS' OPINIONS—You worry about what your family, friends, and colleagues think of you. You fear they'll disapprove of your goals and decisions. You're eager for others' validation and hesitate to take action if you don't have it.

LACK OF FOCUS—You're distracted. Your mind wanders. You're exposed to so many opportunities that you're unsure where to devote your attention. You're anxious to do *something* but can't figure out what you should do.

PERFECTIONISM—You want to be flawless. You're

concerned about making mistakes or overlooking details that'll come back to haunt you. You put enormous pressure on yourself to be perfect. This expectation makes every action seem daunting, which causes you to procrastinate.

FIXATION ON PERFECT TIMING—You wait for the perfect time to act. You count on circumstances to line up just the right way before you put your plans in motion. You watch for ideal conditions to maximize your chances of success and minimize the likelihood of failure. But such conditions never surface, and you never take the first step.

Do any of these reasons for inaction ring true for you? Do any of them hit close to home? If so, don't worry. I'll show you how to build your "take purposeful action" habit and short-circuit these tendencies in the process.

How to Build Your Action Habit

The most important thing you can do from the outset is to set your expectations regarding the results of your efforts. Success isn't guaranteed in any endeavor. And even when success occurs, the road leading to it is often fraught with setbacks and complications. Anticipate them. Plan for them. The only way to ensure that your path will be trouble-free is to wait for perfect conditions and the certainty of your outcome. The problem is that if you wait for these things, you'll never take the first step.

Once you've set your expectations, commit to taking the initiative. Resolve to take action *with intention*. This sounds simple, but it's a crucial step that's easy to overlook. If you neglect to make this commitment at the start, you'll be vulnerable to the temptation to quit when things don't go your way.

These preliminary measures put you in the right frame of mind for what follows. Now, we're ready to cover a few hands-on, tangible things you can do daily to develop and reinforce your action habit.

Think About Your End Goal

It's easy to lose sight of your desired outcome. It's easy to forget *why* you're doing what you're doing. This tactic will prevent you from getting bogged down in the details and losing track of the bigger picture.

Reflect on your intended result each day. Ideally, do it several times each day. Take a moment to think about your objective with absolute clarity. What *precisely* do you want to accomplish? What does success look like to you? How does it feel? How will it change your life? The more you think about these things in a crystal-clear manner, the more tangible your end goal will seem.

Create a Detailed Roadmap

To take purposeful action, you must know precisely what to do. You need a roadmap that presents a clear path to success. This map should include every step you need to take to accomplish what you're setting out to do.

Keeping your end goal in mind, make a list of actions you need to take to get there. No action is too small. In fact, the smaller the better. Small tasks are immediately actionable, unlike large tasks, and that's perfect for building an action habit.

Let's suppose you want to start a business. You'll need to research and validate the product or service you envision providing. You'll need to evaluate the competition and determine the market demand. You'll need to create plans related to marketing, branding, operations, and finances. You'll need to consider legal matters, including how to structure your business and acquire licenses. You'll need to think about hiring people, reaching out to potential suppliers, and providing customer support.

There are many steps involved, and they can be daunting to the point that you're left unable to act.

Break down these large items into tiny tasks you can do in a few minutes. For example, here's a list of small, purposeful actions to take in the process of researching and validating your business idea:

- Look online for businesses that offer a product or service similar to the one you want to provide. Bookmark them to review them later.
- Do keyword research to determine how difficult it will be to rank well on Google.
- Ask friends, family, and coworkers about whether they'd be interested in the product or service you want to offer.
- Check online review-oriented sites (e.g., Yelp, Amazon, etc.) to identify common complaints and pain points.
- Design simple polls on social media to gauge interest.
- Create Google Alerts to keep you updated on trends related to your idea.
- Subscribe to newsletters or magazines related to your idea.

There are dozens of tasks involved in this stage of starting a business. When you break your goal down this way, you give yourself an extensive list of small things you can do in a few minutes. The smaller the task and the more quickly you can complete it, the more encouraged you'll be to get it done.

Complete One Task Each Day

You have your roadmap in hand. You've deconstructed your end goal into a long list of tiny actions you'll need to take to make forward progress. You know everything that needs to be done to accomplish what you're trying to do.

Commit to doing one task on your list each day. Put it on your calendar, and assign a small time block (e.g., ten minutes). Mornings work well because that's when your willpower tends to be highest. Whenever you decide to schedule it, each task should take very little time, so it shouldn't impact your day. If the task looks like it'll take longer than a few minutes, break it down further.

For example, suppose that interviewing your friends, family, and coworkers and gauging their interest in your product or service is likely to take an hour. Break down this task by listing each person you intend to interview. Each interview should only take a few minutes.

Suddenly, you're no longer just dreaming about your goal. You're taking small steps toward accomplishing it. While the tasks you're completing may seem far removed from your goal, you're taking action every day. Purposeful action. Intentional action. And you're doing so as part of your daily routine.

That's how you build and reinforce this habit. That's how you ensure that it sticks.

As your action habit develops, you'll feel like doing more than one task daily. Follow this impulse. Do two each day. Then, graduate to doing three each day. You have your roadmap. You set the pace. What matters most is that you're developing one of the most important habits you can build in the context of thinking big.

EXERCISE #7

CHOOSE A SMALL GOAL. Then, break it down into a list of tiny actions you can take daily to accomplish it.

For example, suppose you'd like to start a workout routine. You might break it down as follows:

- Define the type of workout (e.g., aerobic, flexibility, strength training, muscle gain).
- Review your options (e.g., yoga, swimming, jogging, high-intensity interval training).
- Determine when you'll work out (6:00 am to 7:00 am, 6:00 pm to 7:00 pm, etc.).
- Decide where you'll work out (gym, garage, nearby park, etc.).
- Research specific exercises and how to perform them correctly.
- Choose a tracking system that records the metrics of each exercise (reps, weights, etc.).
- Enlist a friend to be a "workout buddy."

Notice that each of these tasks can be completed quickly. A few can even be broken down further. For example, you might research one exercise daily instead of multiple exercises. You might even choose to do so over several days, watching instructional videos demonstrating a particular exercise—one video each day.

The point is that you give yourself an easy way to take consistent action toward your goal. The smaller the actions, the more likely you are to take them daily.

Time required: 20 minutes.

STEP 8: BUILD YOUR SUPPORT TEAM

66 Surround yourself with only people who are going to lift you higher.

— OPRAH WINFREY

Training your mind to think big shouldn't be a reclusive, lonesome journey. Just because you have bold ambitions doesn't mean you must walk that path alone. On the contrary, your journey should include others.

You'll want to share your vision with people who will encourage you to aspire to achieve extraordinary feats. You'll want to express your dreams to those who will boost your morale when you encounter setbacks and celebrate with you when you reach significant milestones.

These individuals form your support team. They'll rally around you and lift your spirits when you feel emotionally depleted. They'll cheer you on and inspire you to press forward when you reach important thresholds. They'll sustain your long-term enthusiasm when urgent matters in the present threaten to distract you.

It's easy to discount the value of surrounding yourself with supportive people. You may even feel that leaning on others is a sign of weakness. That it implies you're inadequate in some way. That you don't measure up. But nothing could be further from the truth. Drawing on others for encouragement, insight, inspiration, and their expertise is a sign of personal and professional maturity.

In short, your support network will be instrumental in your success. But you'll need to recruit the right people for the job.

Who Should Be On Your Support Team?

Generally, anyone who wants to see you succeed should have a place in your corner. This includes your spouse, kids, and other supportive family members. It might also include your friends, colleagues, and neighbors. It can even include folks you've met on your favorite social media platforms. They're delighted to hear about your victories and quick to encourage you when you struggle.

However, specific roles need to be filled on your support team. You'll likely need to look beyond these groups for the right people to fill them. Here are the four most essential roles to fill, along with their respective responsibilities:

1. ACCOUNTABILITY PARTNER—This person will check in periodically to ensure you stay on track. They'll ask you to describe your progress. They'll encourage you to meet your milestones. They'll remind you about the goals you've committed to and spur you to take the necessary actions to achieve them. Your accountability partner will listen to your concerns but do so to nudge you forward.

2. MENTOR—This individual will provide advice and insight gained from experience, including mistakes they've made. They'll have accomplished what you want to achieve and can help you create a roadmap that will lead you to similar results. They'll provide constructive feedback based on their insight and help you avoid hazards they've encountered. You must trust and respect this person because they'll serve as a role model.

3. COACH—This person will help you to remain optimistic and enthusiastic about hitting your milestones and reaching your goals. They'll push you to be more productive and manage your time more effectively so you can get more done. They'll inspire you to be mentally

resilient when things go wrong, and they'll celebrate with you when things go well. Your coach will encourage you to maintain a growth mindset when you face setbacks, building your confidence as you solve problems. A good coach will also urge you to balance your ambitions with your current quality of life so you don't sacrifice the latter while chasing the former.

4. **PEOPLE WITH SIMILAR AMBITIONS**—These folks aspire to accomplish what you want to achieve. They're aware of your challenges and frustrations because they face the same ones. They're mindful of the emotions you experience because they experience them, too. They're acquainted with the successes and failures that are a part of your journey because they're also going through them. This group will celebrate with you, commiserate with you, and inspire you to keep pressing forward through a shared experience.

Some of the people on your support team might fill multiple roles. For example, your accountability partner may have the knowledge, experience, and insight necessary to serve as your mentor. This can be beneficial as it can inspire a more profound sense of trust and accountability.

Additionally, multiple people might fill one or more roles. For example, your mentor and coach might share your values and convictions and have similar ambitions. This, too, can be useful as it promotes camaraderie and collaboration.

These four roles, reinforced by a bedrock of supportive family, friends, coworkers, and others, are essential for thinking big and achieving ambitious goals. With this in mind, how do you build your team?

How to Build Your Support Team

First, think carefully about the types of support you'll need to bring your dreams to life. You might need financial support, such as loans, investments, or other types of funding. You may need emotional support, such as people to talk to when you experience setbacks and other frustrations. You'll likely need advice, especially when solving challenging problems and making important decisions. You'll need constructive feedback to help you optimize your approach and make adjustments. You'll need someone to help you stay on track.

If you know someone who has achieved what you aspire to achieve, they can help you brainstorm your support team. Offer to buy them lunch and ask them for suggestions based on their experience.

Once you've identified the types of support you'll need, start building your team. Begin with your friends and loved ones. Share your big goals with them. Explain that you'd like to lean on them occasionally for emotional support. Not everyone will be willing to help you in this way. That's fine. It's better to know this upfront than to lean on them later and find out they're unavailable.

Think about your other relationships. You may already know people who can fill one or more roles we discussed earlier.

For example, suppose you'd like to start a law firm with multiple partners. Do you know other lawyers who've done this successfully? Do you know people who operate successful partnerships in other fields? They can provide insight unique to launching and running this business structure.

You probably know someone who'll agree to keep you accountable. This individual might be a close friend, a past business partner, or even someone you've never met in person and know only through social media.

You may have colleagues who have been successful in their fields and are now retired. Even if their fields of expertise are unrelated to your ambitions, these people can serve as coaches. They know what it takes to succeed and are familiar with the attendant challenges.

Once you've exhausted your close personal relationships, look beyond them. For example, you can meet like-minded folks by attending conferences and seminars related to your goals. You can join professional organizations. You can meet people with similar interests and ambitions on Facebook and LinkedIn. You can reach out to your school's alums, particularly if their fields of study match your own. Speak to your colleagues and coworkers; you may discover their aspirations align with yours. Ask people you know to introduce you to people *they* know.

All of the above are opportunities to identify and recruit people who can become an integral part of your support team. Some of these methods may feel uncomfortable, particularly when they involve meeting new people. But that unease will evaporate once you establish trust and rapport with them.

How to Handle Unsupportive People

One risk of sharing your ambitions with others is that some people will be unsupportive. Their lack of support can manifest in many ways. Some will not understand why you want to achieve what you're striving toward. Some will show disinterest or indifference. Some will be cynical or pessimistic. Some may actively undermine you. Some may be downright hurtful.

Their reasons will vary, ranging from aloofness to jealousy. What matters is that you interact with them in a way that allows you to continue thinking big without jeopardizing your optimism and self-belief. Here are three tactics that will help.

Tactic #1: Accept Their Lack of Support

When friends and loved ones express confusion or apathy, it's tempting to want to persuade them to support you. You're excited about your plans and endeavors, and you want them to be excited, too. But this is usually a waste of time and energy.

Accept that others may not understand. Accept that they might be uninterested in what you want to accomplish. Accept that they don't support you in the way you hope they will. Once you embrace this reality, you can focus your time and energy where it'll do far more good.

Tactic #2: Set Communication Boundaries

Once you've identified unsupportive people in your life, refrain from discussing your plans and goals with them. If they ask, deflect and change the subject. If they persist, explain that you'd prefer not to talk about your aspirations because they've proven unsupportive of them.

They might be taken aback. They might feel offended. That's okay. You are only responsible for communicating with grace, respect, and tact. You are not responsible for how they receive and react to your message.

Tactic #3. Focus on Your Tribe

You've created your support team, the small group of individuals who fill specific roles. Additionally, you'll know—or meet—people who aren't a part of this team but are similar to you in some way. They are fellow big thinkers. They have goals that might differ entirely from yours but possess the same enthusiasm and passion. They share your excitement and zeal. This is your tribe. They are your community.

You'll share ideas with them. You'll encourage each other. You'll find their energy to be infectious. The more time you spend with your community of other big thinkers, the less you'll be bothered by unsupportive people.

We'll talk more about this in the next section.

EXERCISE #8

THIS IS A BRAINSTORMING EXERCISE. Its purpose is to spur you to consider your resources. You'll identify candidates who are qualified to fill each of the four roles described above.

If you prefer, you can do this in the old-fashioned way, with a pen and paper. I recommend doing it digitally. That way, you can easily make notes and move names around as you see fit.

Create the following four column headings:

1. Accountability partner
2. Mentor
3. Coach
4. People with similar ambitions

Underneath each heading, write down the names of people you know who might be qualified to serve in that particular capacity. Start with friends and family members. Then, expand your list of possibilities by considering your coworkers, colleagues, and acquaintances. Next, think of past bosses, professors, collaborators, and business partners.

Once you've reviewed the people you know personally, consider the people you know online. This includes those you've connected with on social media sites, forums, and other online communities.

Next, consider people you don't know but could easily reach out to. This might include local business leaders, fellow members of professional associations, and friends of friends. Remember, you're only one introduction away from finding the perfect candidate for your support team.

The final step is approaching the people on your list and pitching them about being on your team. Don't dance around the topic. Be clear, concise, and earnest.

You'll quickly get an impression of who is willing to help.

One quick note: Avoid assuming others don't want to be on your support team. Unless you're sure someone doesn't want to participate, consider them a candidate (if they're qualified). Serving as an accountability partner, coach, or mentor can be a deeply rewarding experience. Many people would jump at the chance to help if they knew others were seeking that support. So, present the opportunity and let them respond to it.

Time required: 20 minutes.

STEP 9: SPEND TIME WITH ACCOMPLISHED BIG THINKERS

> The fastest way to change yourself is to hang out with people who are already the way you want to be.
>
> — REID HOFFMAN

Motivational speaker Jim Rohn once said, "You're the average of the five people you spend the most time with." While this statement oversimplifies the influence others have on our decisions and actions, it contains a kernel of truth. The people who are closest to us *do* influence us. They affect our attitudes and behaviors. We celebrate our uniqueness but also mirror those with whom we feel a kinship via shared experiences, beliefs, and aspirations.

This influence can manifest in many ways, both negative and positive. It can fuel behaviors like the bystander effect, which asserts people are less inclined to help someone in immediate need when others are nearby. It can also take the form of peer pressure, prompting a host of bad decisions and self-sabotaging behaviors.

This influence can also serve as a catalyst for personal growth and achievement. When you spend significant time with people who have accomplished remarkable things, you begin to adopt their mindset and outlook. Their enthusiasm becomes contagious. Their confidence becomes inspiring. Their optimism becomes irresistible.

My friend Dale is a perfect example. He epitomizes enthusiasm, confidence, and optimism. He also embraces intentionality (positivity will only get you so far). He's a big thinker and takes action aggressively. I've watched him build multiple businesses from scratch, one of them a 7-figure enterprise. His progress and success often seem to materialize through the sheer force of his will.

Dale's influence on my mindset and attitude has been life-changing.[1] Spending time with him helped me to purge my cynicism, pessimism, and timidity and replace them with hopefulness, idealism, and boldness about what I can accomplish. His big thinking fuels my own.

But there's much more to this than fostering a positive mindset and "can do" attitude. You'll reap a lot of other practical, useful benefits when you spend time with high-achieving big thinkers.

Why You Should Surround Yourself With Successful Big Thinkers

In the preceding chapter, we discussed the role of a mentor on your support team. These individuals have succeeded in their fields and can offer crucial insight and wisdom gained from their hard-won experience. But they don't have to be formal team members for you to reap the rewards of interacting with them.

When you associate with successful people, you see things from a broader perspective. You interpret challenges differently. You tackle problems more creatively. You recognize opportunities that had previously gone unnoticed.

High-achieving individuals also tend to make decisions assertively. They rarely procrastinate. They don't hem and haw. They analyze situations, consider their resources, and take purposeful action. Being around people like this will encourage you to adopt similar behaviors.

Successful big thinkers can also help you to refine your expectations. They can detail their successes and explain their impact, which might be different than you imagine. They can share their failures and describe how these events affected their outlook and prompted them to modify their approach. Hearing their stories can change how you perceive success and failure. It can shape your interpretation of both as you press forward toward achieving your ambitions.

High achievers know people who can help you. They can introduce you to a broader network of individuals who can offer advice, insight, and a plethora of resources. This introduction can have a ripple effect as this broader network leads to making connections with others.

Successful big thinkers can also help you to improve your social skills. Their success usually stems — at least in part — from their relationships. They know how to interact with others. How to inspire. How to lead. How to communicate. They know how to build trust and resolve conflicts. How to ask good questions and listen carefully to the responses. How to collaborate and motivate. When you spend time with these individuals, you learn these skills. There's no better way to learn them than by observing them in action.

To wrap up, associating with high achievers will improve your mindset and attitude. Plus, you'll find they'll usually be very supportive of your goals and ambitions. But as we've discussed, there's so much more you stand to gain from seeking and nurturing these relationships. The question is, how do you approach these people?

How to Approach Successful Big Thinkers

Approaching people who have accomplished extraordinary things is intimidating. It can feel as if you're intruding on their space. You might even compare your achievements with theirs and feel you don't measure up. Don't be discouraged.

The most important thing to remember is that these concerns reflect how you feel about yourself. They echo your self-image. They don't reflect how the people you want to approach think of you. They don't know anything about you, so they haven't formed a strong impression yet.

Sure, you may encounter folks who are unpleasant— obnoxious even. But you'll find that most will be approachable, friendly, and eager to learn about your ambitions.

I met Dale at a coffee shop. I had seen him there several weekends and grew curious about him. He always had his laptop with him and gave off an entrepreneurial vibe. (Later, I learned he was running a successful business while maintaining his corporate job.)

So, one day, I approached him. I set aside my inhibitions, mustered my courage, and introduced myself. We ended up enjoying a long, engaging conversation during which we learned more about each other. We started to meet up each weekend. Then he quit his corporate job, and we began to meet up regularly each week.

That was many years ago. While the coffee shop is now gone, my relationship with Dale has continued to deepen. He has become one of my main confidantes, a person I turn to regularly for advice, ideas, and inspiration when I struggle.

Here's my point: if you feel intimidated by someone

you want to approach, remind yourself that they don't know you (yet). Your feelings don't inform their impression of you. Moreover, successful big thinkers are curious about other people. They'll want to meet you. They'll want to learn more about you and hear about your goals and plans. After you build trust with them, they might become an invaluable part of your circle.

With that in mind, here are a few tips you can use to approach and connect with high achievers successfully.

Simplify Your Purpose

Your goal is to meet them. Don't worry about what happens afterward. Don't worry about getting advice, feedback, and insight from them. Forget about interviewing them, networking with them, and collaborating with them. Set aside thoughts about what they can do for you. Instead, focus on introducing yourself.

Simplifying your purpose makes it easier to take action. When you have this single objective in mind, you're less susceptible to negative self-talk. You may still experience anxiety. But it's easier to control.

Investigate Your "Target"

Learn something about them. What do they do for a living? What type of success have they achieved? What challenges have they encountered and overcome? What are their values? What do they stand for?

These days, you can learn a lot about successful people online. You can see their career path on LinkedIn, including the companies they've worked for (or operated) and the positions they've held. You can read articles they've written on their blogs, LinkedIn, and Medium. You can watch videos they've published on YouTube. You can get an impression of their personalities and values by following them on Twitter and subscribing to their newsletters.

A single nugget of information can be the perfect catalyst for saying hello to a high-achieving big thinker.

Plan Your Approach

Don't wing it. Don't rely on your ability to think on your feet. Figure out what you'd like to say in advance. Otherwise, you might find yourself in an awkward position (e.g., "Hi, I'm Damon. Umm, I like your tie.")

Outline your talking points, keeping things simple and concise. Here's a basic plan:

- Introduce yourself.
- Briefly mention what you're working toward.
- Compliment them on something they've done that relates to your goals (even tangentially).
- Express your admiration.
- Seek permission to contact them in the future.

I'll give you an example I used while writing my first

book. At the time, I was comfortable writing but knew little about how to release and market books. So, I did a bit of research. I identified a prolific author whose books regularly hit the bestseller lists. Here's the email I sent him (I've changed his name for privacy):

Hi Chris,
My name is Damon. I'm a budding author writing my first book. I plan to write several more.

I've read and enjoyed many of your books. I noticed that they always hit the bestseller lists. As someone who is just getting started, I find that remarkable.

Would you be open to my reaching out to you for a tip or two on how to launch when I'm ready to publish?

All the best,
Damon

You'll notice that my email sticks closely to the basic plan I outlined above. It's simple and concise. But did it work?

"Chris" responded within a few hours (!) and invited me to contact him in the future. He was incredibly kind and welcoming, instantly putting my fears about approaching him to rest. Since then, we've spoken many times, and he's provided me with sage advice regarding several aspects of writing and publishing books.

Bottom line: Don't be intimidated by the thought of approaching accomplished big thinkers. They're just people like you and me. They have similar fears and doubts. They deal with similar challenges and setbacks. They feel proud and gratified when someone recognizes their achievements. Most importantly, like most people, they enjoy connecting with others, particularly those with whom they share something in common.

You have to approach them to spend time with them. The good news is that, like any new practice, the more you do it, the easier it gets. Do it consistently, and you'll eventually find yourself surrounded by high achievers who dream big and aim high by instinct. And you might just be shocked by how inspiring and uplifting these relationships can be.

∾

EXERCISE #9

∾

This exercise has three parts. First, pick one successful big thinker you know. Learn more about them online. Search for them on the sites mentioned above (LinkedIn, Medium, Twitter, etc.). Then, do a simple Google search using their name.

Second, craft an email that follows the basic plan I described earlier. Use something you've discovered about the person you're reaching out to (ideally, an accomplishment) as the driving force.

Third, send the email.

The worst that can happen is that they fail to respond, and even *that* may not imply anything. Perhaps they didn't see your email.[2] Maybe they're swamped. Maybe they're on vacation. If you don't hear back from them, you can always follow up later.

The primary purpose of this exercise is to improve your approach. It's the first step toward building a solid network of high-achieving big thinkers who will encourage you to believe in yourself and keep pressing forward.

Time required: 30 minutes.

---

1. In my less humble moments, I entertain myself by thinking I've had a similar effect on him. Dale is a member of my support team, and I'm a member of his. This symbiotic relationship is a testament to the value and importance of having supportive people in your corner.
2. I can tell you from experience that this can happen easily. It has happened to me many times over the years.

STEP 10: PUT FAILURE TO IMMEDIATE USE

 I have always learned more from my failures
and therefore I was never afraid of failure.

— ARNOLD SCHWARZENEGGER

Failure is a brutal teacher. But if you're open to
its lessons, it will make you more resilient,
aware, creative, and determined. It will reveal
what works and what doesn't. It will encourage you to
reflect on your results and examine the decisions and
actions that produced them. It will inspire you to experiment and test new tactics and strategies. Failure is feedback that can help you improve every area of your life.

But to take advantage of these benefits, you must put

failure to use. You have to take action on it. The more quickly you do so, the better. Otherwise, the lessons, insights, and impetus for reflection erode. The opportuni ties for personal growth and development fade. They weaken as time passes.

One of the main themes of this book is that thinking big with intention involves more than just thinking. It requires *doing*. It requires making decisions and taking action purposefully. As mentioned earlier, that's what separates thinking big from dreaming.

Below, I'll show you how to take advantage of the wisdom and knowledge you gain when you come up short. I'll show you how to leverage both to constantly work in your favor.

This is the final step toward reframing how you perceive the world and the opportunities it presents. It's the last phase in changing how you see your potential for achieving your most ambitious goals and accomplishing extraordinary things. But first, let's summarize the rewards that failure can offer you.

Failure Makes You Better (If You Let It)

The moment you commit to seeing failure as an opportunity to learn, grow, and improve, it becomes less scary. You'll feel less anxious about the possibility that you might stumble and miss your mark. When you see failure in a positive light, it becomes a source of encouragement for what it teaches rather than what it seems to condemn.

It no longer bruises your ego. It no longer injures your pride.

Instead, it inspires you to bounce back and do better. It gives you the clarity and awareness to *be* better. It makes you...

MORE ADAPTABLE—When you try something, and it fails, you have an opportunity to adjust your approach. You adapt by trying something different. The more you do this, the more flexible and resourceful you become.

MORE RESILIENT—Each time you encounter adversity and persevere, you desensitize your brain from future setbacks. Future challenges become less discouraging, and you become more inclined to endure and stick it out.

MORE TENACIOUS—The more resilient you become, the more determined you become to forge ahead. You gain confidence in your ability to overcome adversity. You train yourself to keep striving and never give up.

MORE CREATIVE—Failure introduces problems that must be solved before you can move forward. It encourages you to experiment with potential solutions. It emboldens you to embrace new perspectives and thinking patterns that can help you to conquer obstacles.

MORE SELF-REFLECTIVE—Failure is a surefire cure for hubris. It makes you aware of your weaknesses. It highlights your shortcomings. It reveals your blind spots. All of these insights are positive if you have a growth mindset.

MORE EMPATHETIC—When you try something that fails,

you learn to be more compassionate toward others when *they* fail. You enjoy a rapport fueled by your experience. You can put yourself in their shoes and support them rather than judge them.

MORE APPRECIATIVE—Every failure reminds you not to take success for granted. It encourages you to appreciate your past accomplishments and recognize the planning, diligence, and creativity they required of you. It also prompts you to reflect on the personal and professional growth you've enjoyed during your journey.

Failure is a stern, uncompromising, and sometimes unforgiving instructor. It teaches difficult, unpleasant lessons. But the education comes with life-changing rewards. If you put them to use, they'll help you achieve remarkable things you once believed were beyond your abilities.

How to Use Failure to Your Advantage

Success feels better than failure, of course. It's more gratifying. More empowering. More inspiring. But it doesn't present as many opportunities for personal and professional growth. Success can give you momentum but rarely teaches you anything substantive about yourself. It doesn't promote self-reflection, so it seldom leads to improved self-awareness.

While failure is disappointing and discouraging, it can

also be your greatest ally. Here are several ways you can put it to immediate use.

Figure Out What Went Wrong

When you don't get the results you desire, review your process to learn why. Go through each step and try to determine the contributing factors.

- Was your objective unclear?
- Was your objective too difficult, given your circumstances?
- Did you neglect to prepare correctly?
- Did you overlook essential resources that you needed to succeed?
- Did you use your resources in an unsustainable way?
- Was your execution flawed?
- Did you make hasty decisions with insufficient information?
- Did you deviate from a proven procedure?

Failure always leaves clues. You may be tempted to ignore them and press onward because taking action feels productive. Resist the temptation. Pause and reflect. Investing time now to figure out why things went wrong will help you avoid repeating the same mistakes. It will save you a lot of time and frustration.

Identify Controllable Variables

As you investigate the causes of your failure, you'll notice that some are within your power to influence, and some are entirely beyond your control. It's crucial to make this distinction as early as possible. Otherwise, you'll waste significant time, energy, and attention fretting over things you can do nothing about.

Here are some elements that are within your control:

- New skills you can learn.
- How you manage your resources.
- Your decision-making process.
- The specificity of your plans.
- Your work ethic.
- Your commitment.
- How you respond to challenges.

Here are some over which you have zero control:

- The weather.
- The economy.
- Other people's decisions.
- Unfortunate timing.
- Government regulations.
- Access to resources.
- Cultural trends.

The above is just a small sampling to help you distinguish between the two groups. Remember, agonizing over things you can't influence meaningfully does no good. But if any of these things contributed to your lack of success, now is the time to make that determination.

Take Corrective Action

If, during your review, you discover that you fell short because of factors you control, you can now adjust your strategy. You can make new plans based on this insight. For example, you might:

- Fill gaps in your knowledge.
- Expand your skill set.
- Change how you allocate your resources.
- Identify *better* resources.
- Adjust the timing of your efforts.
- Improve how you track your progress.
- Refine your decision-making process (e.g., how you gather information, evaluate options, and assess risks).

When you investigate the factors contributing to your failure, you unlock a treasure trove of insight. But you must *act* on this insight to use it to your advantage.

Improve Your Mental Game

Your frame of mind is pivotal to this entire journey. It shapes how you perceive yourself, your talents and abilities, and your capacity for success. It determines whether you think you *deserve* success. Your thoughts govern how you react to setbacks and influence whether you give up or persevere. They also shape how you interpret and solve problems.

When you fail, nurture your mental state. Show yourself compassion. Forgive your mistakes and let them go. Review your temperament in light of your current setback. Pause a moment and recommit to your goals (if they're still relevant).

Now is also the time to double down on your resolve to maintain a growth mindset. Reaffirm your intention to embrace challenges and face them head-on rather than avoid them. Remind yourself that you can acquire practically any knowledge you need and develop virtually any required skill.

This part of Step 10 is essentially a mental fitness program. In the same way you exercise to strengthen your body's muscles, you can employ these steps to strengthen your mental game. And it can make all the difference as you pursue your inevitable success.

WE'VE SPENT a lot of time discussing failure in this book. That's for good reason. How you perceive failure, interpret its message, and respond to its lessons will determine how it influences your mindset. It will decide whether you use failure to your advantage, fueling your enthusiasm, motivation, and resilience, or allow it to dishearten you, shake your resolve, and undermine your ambitions.

How you grapple with failure, harness it, and ultimately capitalize on it is intrinsic to thinking big. It forms the core of the mental framework you're building. It's an integral part of training yourself to aspire to greatness and be confident in your ability to learn, adapt, and overcome any obstacle in your path.

EXERCISE #10

LIKE EXERCISE #1, this final exercise has two parts. Both are simple and easy. The first part will help you to reframe how you see failure. The second part will reinforce this change in perspective.

Part I

Recall an occasion where you tried to accomplish something but missed the mark. Your results failed to meet your expectations. First, remember the emotions you felt at the time. Acknowledge them. Were you disappointed? Embarrassed? Angry? Frustrated? Write them down.

Because time has passed, your negative feelings have likely faded. They sting less today, allowing you to see the incident more objectively.

Next, write down five insights you gained from this event. For example, suppose you had a meeting with your boss, and it went poorly. Maybe you weren't prepared for the meeting. Perhaps you didn't arrive with a clearly defined objective. Maybe you communicated in an unclear or combative way.

You control these things. That means you can adjust your approach. You can revise your plan and incorporate different methods, tactics, and practices. You can grow from the experience, personally and professionally, and even take corrective action.

Part 2

Keep a journal in which you record occasions when you fall short. For each entry, list three to five insights you gained from the incident. No insight is too small to be included. And don't dismiss any just because they seem overly simple or obvious.

Each entry you make will reinforce your new perspective on failure. You can refer to your journal for motivation and inspiration as it grows.

One last note: although you can call it your "Failure Journal" if you prefer, I recommend calling it your "Growth Opportunities Journal."

Time required for Part 1: 10 minutes.
Time required for Part 2: 5 minutes per entry.

FINAL THOUGHTS ON THINKING BIG

∾

B y reading *THINK BIG*, you've tapped into a potent source of personal empowerment. It gives you the agency to set your sights higher, make ambitious plans, and live the way you choose. You now possess the autonomy to pursue your dreams without feeling bound by others' expectations. You have the freedom to focus on your ability to learn, grow, adapt, and accomplish things in the future that seem infeasible today.

This new perspective on your talents, strengths, abilities, and capacity for success changes everything:

- It will reprogram your thought patterns.
- It will transform your attitude.
- It will guide your behavior.

- It will reshape your worldview.
- It will encourage you to reframe how you see yourself.
- It will inspire you to redefine who you are and want to become.
- It will catalyze and fuel unshakeable self-belief.

Your mindset affects every aspect of your life, whether you try to make it so or not. It not only governs your day-to-day experiences but also dictates situations and conditions that have a longer-term impact:

- It determines the goals you pursue and the feats you accomplish.
- It influences how your relationships grow and evolve — or wane if you decide to step back from them.
- It shapes how you respond to helpful feedback as well as hurtful criticism.
- It governs your emotional health when you encounter setbacks and challenges.
- It decides the degree of influence your inner critic has over you.
- It affects how you interpret problems, how you learn and adapt, and how you overcome them.

Whether you think big or small is entirely up to you.

That's terrific news because it puts you squarely in the driver's seat. *You* decide your destination. *You* choose the path you'll take to get there. *You* determine where your journey leads and where it ends.

Will you abandon inconsequential undertakings, set your sights higher, and chase your dreams? Will you pursue extraordinary results in your personal and professional life? Will you continuously think bigger and strive for better?

The choice is yours. Today marks the beginning of your story. What does the ending look like?

DID YOU ENJOY READING
THINK BIG?

~

T hank you for reading *THINK BIG*. Your time is important, so I greatly appreciate your decision to spend some of it with me. I sincerely hope that you feel the time was well spent.

If you found this book helpful, would you consider leaving a review on Amazon? Your review can be as brief or detailed as you like. One or two short sentences about a tip or section you enjoyed are perfect. It would mean the world to me. Plus, your review will encourage other folks to read *THINK BIG*.

One final note: I plan to release several more books covering various aspects of time management, productivity, and lifestyle design. If you'd like to be notified when I release them (usually at a steep discount), consider joining my mailing list. You'll receive my 40-page PDF ebook titled *Catapult Your Productivity! The Top 10 Habits You Must Develop To Get More Things Done.*

You can join my list at the following address:

https://artofproductivity.com/free-gift/

I'll also send you my best productivity and time management tips via my email newsletter. You'll receive tips and tactics on beating procrastination, creating morning routines, avoiding burnout, and developing razor-sharp focus, along with many other productivity hacks!

If you have questions or want to share a tip, technique, or mind hack that has made a positive difference in your life, please feel free to email me at damon@artofproductivity.com. I'd love to hear about it!

Until next time,

Damon Zahariades
https://artofproductivity.com/

ABOUT THE AUTHOR

Damon Zahariades is a corporate refugee who endured years of unnecessary meetings, drive-by chats with coworkers, and a distraction-laden work environment before striking out on his own. Today, in addition to writing a growing catalog of time management and productivity books, he's the showrunner for the productivity blog ArtofProductivity.com.

In his spare time, he enjoys playing chess, poker, and the occasional video game with friends. And he continues to promise himself that he'll start playing the guitar again.

Damon lives in Southern California with his beautiful, supportive wife and their affectionate, quirky, and sometimes mischievous dog. He's looking wistfully at his 50th birthday in the rearview mirror.

OTHER BOOKS BY DAMON ZAHARIADES

∽

How to Lead a Disciplined Life

The Mental Toughness Handbook

The Procrastination Cure

To-Do List Formula

80/20 Your Life!

The Time Chunking Method

How to Make Better Decisions

The Art of Living Well series

The Art Of Saying NO

The Art of Letting GO

The Art of Finding FLOW

The 30-Day Productivity Boost series

The 30-Day Productivity Plan - VOLUME I

The 30-Day Productivity Plan - VOLUME II

Self-Help Books for Busy People series

Small Habits Revolution

The Joy Of Imperfection

The P.R.I.M.E.R. Goal Setting Method

Improve Your Focus and Mental Discipline series

Fast Focus

Morning Makeover

Digital Detox

Visit ArtofProductivity.com for a complete list of titles and summaries. All titles are available for purchase in ebook, paperback, hardcover, and audiobook formats at ArtofProductivity.com/Amazon.

Printed in Great Britain
by Amazon

50025134R00099